ID0625168

Goalkeeping
the specialist

Goalkeeping
the specialist

DAVID COLES

The Crowood Press

First published in 2003 by
The Crowood Press Ltd
Ramsbury, Marlborough
Wiltshire SN8 2HR

www.crowood.com

© David Coles 2003

All rights reserved. No part of this publication may be reproduced or
transmitted in any form or by any means, electronic or mechanical,
including photocopy, recording, or any information storage and retrieval
system, without permission in writing from the publishers.

British Library Cataloguing-in-Publication Data
A catalogue record for this book is available from the British Library.

ISBN 1 86126 592 1

Frontispiece: I would like to thank Paul Jones for the belief and
confidence he has shown in my coaching methods over the past five
seasons that we have worked together. His professionalism and attitude
to everything we have worked towards are unquestionable, which has
made our working relationship most enjoyable.

Designed and typeset by Focus Publishing, 11a St Botolph's Road,
Sevenoaks, Kent TN13 3AJ

Printed and bound in Great Britain by The Bath Press

Contents

Acknowledgements

During the writing of this book I have received the help and support of the Southampton goalkeepers, Paul Jones, Antti Niemi, Alan Blayney, Gareth Williams and Michael Poke, and would like to extend a special thank you to all of them for their assistance. My thanks also go to Mr Rupert Lowe, Chairman of Southampton Football Club, for allowing me the full use of the club's facilities, and to the management team for their support.

Since entering the world of coaching at premier level, I have met and become friends with some tremendous and supportive coaches at other clubs, especially Eric Steele (Aston Villa) and Simon Smith (Newcastle United), who both share my passion and enthusiasm for this specialist role. My thanks are also due to Mervin Day, for whom I have the utmost respect and who advised me to take my U.E.F.A. goalkeeping licenses to become a coach, and to Len Bond (Bondie), my goalkeeping coach during my days at Yeovil Town and someone who has always been there for me throughout my career. Thanks.

I would also like to extend my thanks to Keith Granger for all his help and support with the Southampton Academy keepers and for doing a great job, especially when I have been away and committed with the first-team keepers; and to Adam Sells for the use of Sells goalkeeping gloves in the technical practices.

I must also thank my photographer, Paul Ansell, for his help and professional advice and for arranging the photo shoots, which I hope, will help to demonstrate some of the techniques explained throughout this book

and also to Southampton F.C. photographer Michael Atkelsky for the Premier League action shots. I am grateful also to my copywriter for correcting my grammar and hopefully making this book more understandable for you all.

Last but not least, thank you to my family for accepting (or putting up with) my obsession with goalkeeping, and finally a special mention for my Mother who died during the writing of this book and never got to see the finished product. God bless and keep you.

The author and his 'top three', who put up with his obsession!

Forewords

GORDON STRACHAN (MANAGER, SOUTHAMPTON FOOTBALL CLUB)

There are two kinds of goalkeeping books – those that tell you about the player, and those that tell you about the position. This is a book for those who want to learn the art of goalkeeping rather than learn about the author.

You will find goalkeeping books written by celebrity goalkeepers with higher profiles, but there is no doubt whatsoever that more work and energy has been put into this book by the author than any other book on goalkeeping. David Coles' career has not been littered by success in terms of trophies; his success is measured by the number of people he improves.

If you want a book that tells a few self-promoting anecdotes or sticks the knife into some big names, then this is not the book for you. But if you want to learn the art of being a goalkeeper and to improve your skills and technique, then it is well worth a read.

PAUL JONES (SOUTHAMPTON FOOTBALL CLUB AND WELSH INTERNATIONAL)

This book is excellently written, clearly explained and easy to understand by goalkeepers of all ages. It is an ideal tool for coaches and budding young keepers alike.

On a personal note, I would like to thank Dave for all his help, support and encouragement through thick and thin.

ANTTI NIEMI (SOUTHAMPTON FOOTBALL CLUB AND FINNISH INTERNATIONAL)

There is nothing worse than going into a training session only to find that the goalkeeping coach hasn't done any preparation. Lots of time is wasted and the coach will end up trying to improvise. Dave's sessions are always obviously well prepared and every practice has meaning and reasons why things are done. Full marks for that.

I have never met anyone who is as interested in goalkeeping as Dave is and this includes the goalkeepers. His professionalism transfers to all the keepers and I personally have never enjoyed training as much as I do at the moment. Dave takes and gives a lot of stick, which for me shows that we work well as a goalkeeping unit, providing a great spirit within the Club.

I think this book is just great – it covers all areas of goalkeeping and it is easy reading for all age groups. It is vital that every drill and practice is explained and the reasons given as to why they are done, and this is made very clear throughout the book. Importantly, the mental side of goalkeeping also receives plenty of coverage – self-confidence is vital for any goalkeeper, regardless of what level he plays at.

My overall verdict on this book is that it provides professional, thorough and understandable coverage on goalkeeping, and that goalkeepers and coaches at all levels will have much to gain from it.

Introduction

'One save doesn't make you a great goal-keeper, the same as one mistake doesn't make you a bad one.'

Firstly, I'm not about to rewrite the art of goalkeeping. My aim is to explain how the techniques can be achieved and the tactics implemented into the modern game. Over the past five years of working with premier league keepers, I have certainly learnt a lot and added to my wealth of experience as a goalkeeping coach. Hopefully you will find this book a useful tool in improving your goalkeeping skills, from basic techniques through to implementing drills and routines to develop keepers of all ages.

I have aimed this book not only at the goalkeeping coach, but also at the young goalkeeper with a limited amount of professional training. If any part of the book helps to improve a young keeper in any way or helps a coach with new techniques, then the writing of this book has been worthwhile. After all, we all have our ambitions to succeed and maybe become the next David Seaman, or even an up-and-coming Chris Kirkland.

Over the last ten years, rules for goal-keepers have often changed, with a goalkeeper being used as an additional outfield player, who is expected to be as good with his feet as he is with his hands. But goalkeepers are a different breed from outfield players. They are asked to dive amongst flying boots and are challenged to stop a ball that can be struck at speeds of 80mph. Goalkeepers are often isolated during play and expected to achieve impossible saves to keep the team in the game.

The position of goalkeeper is extremely pressured – while one incredible save may make you the hero, one mistake that lets in a goal just as easily turns you into the villain of the match. All players make mistakes which are usually quickly forgotten, but when a goalkeeper makes a mistake it can get blown out of all proportion, with television showing it time and again, even in slow motion. Young keepers can find this very difficult to accept, whereas experienced keepers will learn from it and put it behind them. All goalkeepers tend to be obsessive about their art, with a desire to become number one. They strive to find consistency on a regular basis in games as well as in training sessions.

So what is this obsession and what makes a top-class goalkeeper?

Well, read on and hopefully my knowledge and experience might help to give you an insight into what is required to succeed as a goalkeeper, while at the same time giving you an insight into the tools required to become a goalkeeping coach.

The following chapters explain the basics of goalkeeping, from starting positions through to the dedication and hard work that all goalkeepers will require if they are to 'play between the sticks'.

The author with the club's international goalkeepers, Paul Jones and Antti Niemi, pictured at St Mary's stadium before the 2003 FA Cup Final in Cardiff. Both 'keepers played in the final.

GK	–	Goalkeeper	**A**	–	Attacker
S	–	Server	**D**	–	Defender
△	–	Cone	**X**	–	Marker disc
C	–	Coach	**O**	–	Ball
——▶	–	Movement of ball	·····▶	–	Movement of GK/player
⬜	–	Manikin	**P**	–	Position

Please note: When carrying out practice sessions, use the coaching points that apply to each individual drill, except where indicated.

Key for diagrams and drills.

CHAPTER 1

The Roles of the Goalkeeper and Coach

THE GOALKEEPER

'A personality with specific mentality that fits the role.'

Without a doubt, the goalkeeper is the most important part of any team (although as a goalkeeper, I may be a little biased!) The role of the keeper is a very specialist one, with a vast amount of responsibility placed on the shoulders of one person. Goalkeepers can either win or loose games, so they must therefore posses certain qualities to play top-level football.

The essential qualities for a goalkeeper are:
• personality
• technical ability
• tactical intelligence
• mental and physical strength
• belief and confidence in personal ability.

Goalkeepers are different to outfield players. When you play football you always want to win, and for an outfield player, winning means scoring goals. Getting the ball in the net is the best feeling in the world for the outfield player. But for the goalkeeper, the reverse applies – you must keep the ball out of the net at all costs. Goalkeepers need a specific type of personality to be able to face the challenges of their role. It takes courage to face the opposition when they are attacking and running at you and you know they will be firing the ball as hard and fast as they can.

Paul Jones in action.

Against all the odds you, the goalkeeper, must throw yourself at the oncoming player's feet, and somehow stop whatever comes at you. Unfortunately, goalkeepers can play brilliantly for 89 minutes of a game, and then in the last minute make one mistake that destroys the whole game. Therefore, as a goalkeeper you must possess all the qualities to suit the needs of the game.

Your instinct should be to win every ball consistently, whether it is in a game or in training, and this will help you to become stronger, both physically and mentally. You should be open minded when being coached or in game-related practice, and be willing to listen and learn from your mistakes at all times.

This education is useful for all up-and-coming keepers, especially where football intelligence is concerned. The goalkeeper can be referred to as the fifth defender in today's game, and becomes the out ball for most defenders, therefore having excellent distribution and supporting qualities to deal with whatever is asked is a must.

Goalkeepers must be able to read the game and influence it to their advantage. It is therefore essential that the keeper understands the team's tactics and is able to adjust accordingly to support play by reading all situations that may arise and by making positive decisions to deal with them. Top-class goalkeepers are the ones that make fewer mistakes; this automatically enables them to compete at the highest level. However, to maintain this level of consistency, there are physical and psychological factors that a goalkeeper needs to possess and maintain.

The necessary physical qualities are:
• height
• reflexes and agility
• speed of movement
• balance and co-ordination.

Goalkeepers are all shapes and sizes – there are no rules set down as to what is the required height or the required shape. However, the first signs of a hardening of opinion appeared when a certain Peter Schmeichel signed for Manchester United and changed the outlook of both managers and goalkeeping coaches alike in the premier league. Height and presence to fill the goal area suddenly became important to all clubs. Defenders can gain added confidence from knowing that the last line of defence is a big target to be beaten.

Added size also gives the goalkeeper a longer reach and an additional advantage when dealing with shots and crosses. However, there are downsides in that some taller keepers don't always attack the crossed ball as they should. Another disadvantage for the larger keeper is that it can be a long way for him to collapse and make the save, whereas the smaller keeper may have more agility and be able to collapse to the ground more quickly. But regardless of size, every keeper will have to perfect all of the techniques in order to succeed.

Speed is an essential part of the goalkeeper's repertoire, not only to deal with shots and 1 v 1 situations, but also for the sweeper–keeper role. But, most importantly, the effective goalkeeper needs speed of mind in order to make quick, positive decisions at the right time. This factor relates to reflexes and agility – a keeper may have to change direction at speed to make a save, especially if defenders deflect the ball or block his vision.

The boss of the eighteen-yard box must always be the goalkeeper, no matter what his size or shape. It is the goalkeeper's role to communicate with and organize defenders in such a way that allows him space to work whilst protecting the goal area. However, not every ball delivered into the eighteen-yard box can be gathered by the keeper. He therefore needs to be able to deliver loud and clear instructions to defenders, in order that they can attempt to deal with the danger early, before it reaches the goalkeeper.

Good communication is often effective and can make a keeper's job easier if he has the vision to anticipate situations early. Both training and match play require the goalkeeper's full attention at all times to guarantee total awareness of what is happening around him. The mental and psychological character of a goalkeeper is important, and should be concentrated on during training sessions so as to improve strength of mind and enhance match performance.

The necessary mental and psychological qualities are:
• bravery
• dedication
• concentration
• positive attitude to training
• positive decision-making abilities.

A goalkeeping coach can train and educate a keeper to the highest standards, but is it very difficult for a coach to make him brave. Courage is paramount in a goalkeeper; he must be prepared to dive at boot level, anticipate and make the right decisions early, as this can limit dangerous build-up play. Being a 'mad goalkeeper' is not an option, but having the courage to dive at someone's feet and to make mistakes in front of 67,000 people is all part of it.

MATCH AND TRAINING PREPARATION

'Luck is when preparation meets with opportunity.'

Mental preparation during training can be achieved by working on the strengths and

Under 10 Academy goalkeeper Stuart Norman showing concentration.

weaknesses of the individual goalkeeper's game.

Confidence plays a major part in the role of a keeper, both technically and tactically. Self-belief will be increased by reviewing the tactical areas of a game during training sessions and by concentrating on a keeper's weaker areas. This will enable the keeper not to be phased by similar circumstances in a match. The effective goalkeeper will aim for perfect practise of the basic skills and techniques through continuous practice and preparation.

In striving for perfection, the coach should recognize the keeper's abilities and praise them accordingly, which will create a positive frame of mind in readiness for a game. However, goalkeepers must create their own mental toughness, to prepare them for the difficult situations that will inevitably arise. This means being able to deal with failure as a result of making mistakes. Playing in this position, one mistake can lead to a goal being scored and this can sometimes, unfortunately, loose you and your team the game. The keeper will often turn to the coach for answers, as to why and how the mistake occurred, and the

*Alan Blayney totally focussed
in training.*

coach must be able to provide the answers. Above all, the coach must not lose faith in the keeper; he must be able to reinforce the positive aspects of the keeper's play, while at the same time analysing any mistakes.

The modern game concentrates on players not as footballers, but as athletes. As a goalkeeper, you must train and prepare throughout the week. However, one mistake in a match can undo a whole week of training and preparation. No one can identify why goalkeepers or even outfield players cannot maintain excellent form week in and week out, except for the fact that nobody is perfect all of the time. Premier league goalkeepers will religiously use an individual pre-match routine, which may become a superstitious ritual before each game. Having this organized set of routines will prepare the keeper in both mind and body, while at the same time helping him to focus and become alert, ready for all eventualities.

One indication of how football has changed over the years is that most top clubs now employ a psychologist to help staff and players alike. These professionals will work with staff to bring out the best in individual players, as well as working with the team collectively. The psychologist's aim is to identify the individual aspirations of each team member while on the field of play. By achieving this, communication throughout the team becomes more open and helps the team to work together as a united force.

*Demonstrating is a big part of
learning at all ages.*

The psychologist is there to help all players, but can provide an added benefit to the goalkeeper by helping him to use mental visualization before a game. The keeper visualizes himself making catches and saves, thereby creating a positive state of mind. In addition, reliving previous situations in the mind will help to enhance a keeper's reactions should a similar situation happen again. Visualization can also be a useful tool if a goalkeeper has made a mistake in previous weeks – negative thoughts may be turned into positive ones by mental correction of the error, helping to restore the keeper's confidence.

The main aspects of psychology to be addressed are:
• confidence-building
• improving concentration
• dealing with competition, mistakes and criticism
• use of goal setting and imagery work.

The ultimate aim for all goalkeepers is to achieve their ideal performance level both mentally and physically.

THE ROLE OF THE GOALKEEPING COACH

'All goalkeeping coaches will bring various aspects of their playing experience and transfer it to their coaching techniques.'

As a coach, when planning sessions you should always consider the number of keepers in your group, their age, ability (if known) and the facilities to hand. All of these factors relate to the safety aspects of a session. It is also important to remember always to use the correct sized ball for each age group. Goalkeepers from nine to eleven years should be training and playing with a size three ball, from twelve to fourteen years use a size four, and from fourteen onwards a size five ball is used.

The coach will introduce the principles of coaching in stages, starting at an introductory level and developing as the goalkeepers progress. By working in stages, the coach can develop techniques to meet the needs and demands of the goalkeepers in every age group. When these areas are identified, the coach can then devise a structured programme of exercise and routine that is both progressive and realistic, in order to enhance the goalkeepers' full potential.

These stages are:
• age
• ability
• experience
• physical development.

The author's pre-match reminders with Antti Niemi.

All premier league clubs employ dedicated goalkeeping coaches at both senior and academy levels. The coach must always be aware of any keeper that is returning to training after an injury. Regardless of whether it is an academy or professional keeper to have been injured, the appropriate departments will assess any injuries and will deal with the necessary requirements and treatments until it is time for the keeper to rejoin the daily work routines. The coach will be advised by the medical team as to the extent of training that the keeper can undergo and for what length of time, until he has been given a clean bill of health.

The coach must be aware of and able to spot an injury, especially with the young keepers, as they may not always admit to having an injury, because all they want to do is play. But this can prolong the recovery process and even cause long-term problems. The coach must maintain a dialogue with the keepers at all times, and persuade them to observe sessions while they are injured; they can still learn by watching and it will help the injured keeper to continue to feel part of the team, so that he does not become restless and irritable.

The manner in which you coach must always be positive. With the professional keepers, the coach must always strive for perfection and keep them on their toes and be consistent throughout their normal routines. With the younger keepers, use question-and-answer sessions that will hopefully help them to evaluate their own mistakes or improve their techniques during games or training.

All sessions must contain a certain amount of command from the coach; after all, you are in charge of the session and you are there to improve the consistency of the keepers. That does not mean shouting for no reason – it means praise when praise is due and diagnosis of mistakes when made. Remember that youngsters' concentration spans can be very erratic, so you may need to

Under 17 keeper Michael Poke listening to what the author has to say!

put on demonstrations more than once, but be patient!

Managers now realize the importance of the specialized role of the goalkeeping coach. It has been said that the goalkeeping coach must have played in goal to be able to coach effectively, and in my experience I believe this to be true. You don't have to have played at the very highest level to be a successful coach, but you must have experienced the highs and lows of the game and have the confidence to teach in all of the five main areas of coaching.

These five areas are:
• motivation
• evaluation
• demonstration
• communication
• fault diagnosis.

It is important that the goalkeeping coach maintains a consistent and methodical approach to training, while at the same time being flexible enough to meet the needs of the individual goalkeeper.

Getting to know your keepers on an individual basis will help you to identify their strengths and weaknesses, so when organising and planning training sessions you can concentrate on these, and incorporate realistic match situations relevant to each of the keepers. Continuous, correct practice will breed self-confidence and the keeper will be rewarded with improved performances. The coach who gains the respect of a keeper will always bring out the best in him.

During the past five years, the Football Association has introduced goalkeeping qualifications that are now recognised worldwide. These are a must for any goalkeeping coach.

The goalkeeping qualifications are:
• UEFA Certificate – Introduction to Goalkeeping
• UEFA B Certificate – Intermediate Goalkeeping
• UEFA A Certificate – Advanced Goalkeeping

TECHNICAL ASPECTS OF COACHING

'Always emphasize quality, not quantity.'

Practice should be specific and measurable as well as time-related. Trying to force an extended session, especially if the goalkeeper is starting to make mistakes, will only destroy confidence. There are three main areas that will contribute to these mistakes, and when this begins to happen the keeper's technique will ultimately suffer.

These areas are:
• trying too hard
• becoming too tired
• reduced confidence.

Always place the emphasis on quality, not quantity, when planning sessions. Technique is the most important aspect of a goalkeeper's game at any level, and continuous work on the basic techniques will improve both the goalkeeper and his match performance.

All faults must be quickly diagnosed with clear and sound knowledge by the coach, who may be required to put on demonstrations, thereby instilling confidence in the keeper by demonstrating his own ability. All goalkeepers will make mistakes during practice, but hopefully the knowledge of the coach will correct these mistakes. It is the coach's job to guide the keeper towards achieving perfect practice and the ultimate result of a clean sheet, and to help the keeper to attain a consistent standard in match performance.

The main areas of goalkeeping techniques at a basic level are competence in catching the ball and appropriate movement so as to be able to react to every situation. One cannot be achieved without the other, so where the feet go, the hands must follow. In fact, it is actually the top half of the body that moves first, with the feet in quick succession. With accurate foot movement into the shot or cross and moving through to the appropriate position, the goalkeeper will have a chance to make a save or catch using the correct handling technique in relation to the ball.

The goalkeeper's aim is to catch the ball, as by doing so he will retain possession and provide an excellent opportunity for the defence to turn and attack, which will be achieved by accurate distribution. However, the goalkeeper's main concern is keeping a clean sheet, which will require the use of all the techniques practised in the training sessions.

These techniques are:
• correct positioning
• assessment and anticipation
• good communication with defenders.

The foundation of all basic techniques is sound footwork and safe handling. If the keeper perfects these elements of the game, he will undoubtedly improve his positioning and catching ability.

The aim of any goalkeeper is a perfect performance on a match day, and working in training sessions on actual situations that occur during games will produce good practice and prepare any goalkeeper to identify and deal with these situations. By working with the defenders, the goalkeeper will form an understanding with them and will establish clear guidelines as to what is required of each other when playing against the opposition, who will have a different set of objectives and may well be playing in a different formation.

Since all goalkeepers are assessed by the mistakes they make, the coach must work on a programme of training and exercise aimed at diminishing the number of errors made by any goalkeeper.

The four main areas that contribute to mistakes are:
• poor technique
• making incorrect decisions
• lack of concentration
• adopting the wrong starting position.

Organizing re-enactments of match situations on a regular basis during training will help the keeper to correct these areas, ultimately resulting in the goalkeeper achieving the required responses and appropriate techniques, and always being prepared for action.

If goalkeepers are to develop their full potential, gaining match experience is paramount, and by observing a keeper's performances on a regular basis the coach will be able to analyse and isolate any weak areas that need improvement.

The author making a flying save in a football league game.

CHAPTER 2

The Goalkeeper

THE YOUNG GOALKEEPER

'Always tailor practice to suit ability.'

Regardless of a goalkeeper's age or level of experience, he will have one specific aim, and that is to keep the ball from entering the net at all costs. When working with young keepers, this will be instilled into them automatically from an early age, and in this respect coaching young keepers will be similar to working with adults. However, the physical and mental strengths of the younger keeper will develop at various stages of growth, and training must be planned in accordance with this.

The muscles and bones of young goalkeepers develop at different rates in line with puberty – these differences in individual development must be treated with the utmost regard by any coach, as incorrect training techniques could have devastating consequences for young keepers. It is common knowledge that muscles are stronger than bones, but they must be developed correctly to prevent tears either to the tendons or ligaments. At the same time, it is important to bear in mind the strength of the growing bones and prevent any damage during growth. In view of this, the coach must tone down the intensity of the training schedules for younger keepers, avoiding prolonged periods of warming-up or excessive exercise drills.

Training methods used for adults should be reassessed and implemented as non-intense sessions suitable for younger keepers. Skills and techniques should be concentrated on rather than fitness levels. The younger keeper will be more affected by weather conditions, so this factor will play a major part in the planning of routines and training sessions. During the heat of summer young keepers can become exhausted and dehydrated very easily and the coach must be aware of this at all times. Equally, during cold spells they should be kept active and involved as much as possible to keep them warm. In both cases, training should be time-related, as children can become tired very easily, especially during periods of growth spurts.

Rest is also an important factor when working with young keepers, whether during or between work sessions and this time can be used for fluid intake to rehydrate in preparation for training. The younger goalkeepers will have limited concentration compared to adults, and if prolonged and intensive drills are coached quality and confidence will suffer. There are several major differences between the young keeper and adult keepers.

Young keepers will have:
• slower decision-making skills
• limitations in retaining information
• slower reactions in different situations
• shorter concentration spans in the earlier age ranges
• an inability to evaluate their performance realistically.

It all begins somewhere. A young Antti
Niemi about to kick-start his career.

- Time-related (length of practice sessions)
- Explanations and demonstrations
- Suitability (age and ability-related)
- Theme (target-specific area)
- Evaluation (open discussion)
- Debrief (praising to maintain confidence).

Young goalkeepers all have different rates at which they develop their skills. Some pick things up very quickly, instinctively learning the correct techniques, but will still need reminding of the need to strive for perfect practice.

The world of football, whether it be premiership clubs or non-league, has scouting systems in place all over the country, including Scotland, Wales and Ireland. Scouts can look for keepers who live no more than an hour and a half in travelling time from the club they represent, and once invited to attend a trial, a young keeper can be given a placement with a club for up to six weeks. It is always difficult for the new triallist goalkeepers who have been invited to work with academy keepers. Though it is an exciting experience, they will often find that their standards are a little behind in terms of knowledge of correct practice, but this can be quickly rectified.

There will always be a settling-in period for young keepers and it can take two to three weeks before they are able to relax and feel comfortable with their surroundings and get used to working with the other keepers. New young keepers can find the academy set-up a little daunting at first, as they will be conscious of the fact that the coaches will be looking for good, up and coming keepers, and that most clubs generally only keep two goalkeepers at each age level. But remember that a young goalkeeper's standard will increase with every session, as will a coach's expectations. Always assess and increase the learning curve to suit the needs of the goalkeeper's abilities.

Training schedules should be tailored around the age and ability of the young keeper. Between the ages of nine and sixteen years the sessions should not exceed more than 90 minutes in total. This should include both warm-up and warm-down sessions, which should be kept to around 15 minutes for each. The quality of service to the goalkeeper is important and poor service will only prolong your drills – providing good quality of service ultimately creates quality in your goalkeeper. When implementing sessions I use the acronym T.E.S.T.E.D., which helps me to emphasize and achieve my aims and goals for the young keepers:

*Stuart Norman preparing
for action.*

Allowing for a settling-in period, the young keepers will be watched and assessed on their strengths and weaknesses and will undertake structured training programmes to help develop their skills. What cannot be promised during these six weeks is that the triallist will eventually be taken on to play for the academy in his age group.

The structure for academies is that keepers between the ages of nine and sixteen are classed as academy keepers, which means working with the club at least three times a week and playing games on a Sunday against other academy teams. From the ages of sixteen to nineteen they become scholars, and will have to undergo training every day, at the same time as continuing with further educational work. This is a safeguard for the future, as professional opportunities can be few and far between – not everyone can make it to the top. After the age of nineteen, if a keeper is selected by the club, he may be offered a professional contract, which will hopefully be the first step towards becoming a reserve team player with the aspiration of joining the first team eventually.

Rejection for youngsters is always difficult to handle, especially at such young ages. The coach should always try to reinforce rejection with positive aspects and an assessment of what areas the young player needs to concentrate on to help him to develop in the future. As with any sport, parents can be very supportive and this will always help with additional encouragement for the future.

It is obviously the decision of the manager who plays, and who is ready to join the first team. To make it this far requires continuous hard work, which will continue throughout the goalkeeper's career.

THE EXPERIENCED GOALKEEPER

'Once the goalkeeper crosses that white line, he will live and die by his own decisions.'

The responsibilities of a premier league goalkeeper are unlike those of any other player in the team. If an outfield player makes a mistake, there will be a good chance that a teammate will rectify the error, but when a goalkeeper makes an error he is usually on his own and it can become a costly mistake. Goalkeepers will react in one of three ways when they have made an error.

These reactions are:
1. The keeper's confidence may become deflated. The opposition will try to benefit by taking advantage of the keeper's nervous state of mind, and even his own teammates may lose faith in his ability.
2. The keeper may over-compensate. This could result in a keeper involving himself in situations where his judgement becomes rash – he may take risks in an attempt to redeem himself.
3. The keeper stays calm and maintains his concentration. Staying calm after a mistake will help the keeper to stay focused and not let the mistake affect his game.

OPPOSITE: *The legendary Peter Schmeichel.*

These are all natural reactions that goalkeepers will experience, but the first two situations can be costly and may lead to further errors. All goalkeepers will make mistakes at some point, and it is how they are dealt with that counts. Having the right temperament is a major requirement for a top-level goalkeeper.

The needs of top-class goalkeepers are very demanding and training must be designed to deal with every situation that may arise in a game. In addition, the goalkeeper can become prone to injury, as specific movements will be explosive and fast in order to assess and counteract the attacking player's next move. All these facts must be considered when organizing and coaching the training sessions.

Until recently, goalkeepers worked in isolation from the rest of the team, only now and again becoming involved in practice such as shooting and crossing, but this has now changed. Goalkeeping drills are mainly functional sessions to begin with, and are then developed into phases of play, small-sided games or full-scale 11 v 11, depending on the club tactics. This will involve the players working with or against the goalkeeper in match situations. I personally like to spend an hour with a keeper working on his technical skills before joining the rest of the team and then continue working on the tactical aspects of the game. The quality time a coach spends with the keeper before joining the rest of the team will help to achieve the following aspects.

- physical and agility work
- specific drills in relation to technique
- psychological and mental preparation.

When these aims and targets have been achieved during training both individually and collectively, then the keeper can move on and continue practising with the rest of the team and working on the tactical side of the game. At this stage of training, goalkeepers will also benefit from taking on the role of an outfield player, as this will enable them to perfect their touch and use their lesser foot more often.

With distribution being such an important part of goalkeeping, assuming the role of an attacking player enables a keeper to gain an insight of play from the other side of the area. It enables him to read the game more clearly and take up positions to counteract the attack. Psychologically, this role-reversal will help a keeper to respond quicker when similar positions of attack are used against him during a game. He will also gain a fuller understanding of play from the outfield.

As a coach, guidance, care and quality time off the field with your goalkeepers are just as important as the training sessions. It will give your keepers time to assess their performance in games and even how they are coming on in training. In my experience, you will be sought out by the keepers and asked for your thoughts. Usually this will happen after they have had time to analyse their game and reflect on their performance.

I would not recommend debriefing or diagnosing a keeper's performance immediately after a game, as this can have a negative effect on the keeper, especially if he has only made one mistake within a generally solid game. When a keeper realizes and admits a mistake, he needs encouragement and confidence-building to prepare for the next game. Give your keepers ways and means of putting the mistake right, first technically and then mentally. Ask open-ended questions, and remember when criticizing to be constructive rather than aggressive. Try to agree on both long-term and short-term objectives.

Without a doubt, an essential part of a coach's role is evaluation of goalkeepers and encouraging them to assess their own strengths and weaknesses in every game as well as in training. Once they can do this, the keepers will be able to identify areas that need extra work in order to improve their game. Assessing and evaluating faults will help keepers to learn from their mistakes, thereby eliminating negative thoughts that would be detrimental to their performance.

From a goalkeeping coach's point of view, reassurance is a positive reaction, which will help a keeper to recover from a mistake more quickly. You will be the first person a keeper turns to in a crisis, so make it clear that you are there to talk things through. Self-diagnosis is healthy, and with the coach asking open-ended questions, hopefully the goalkeeper will come to understand and rectify his mistakes. It is imperative that the keeper retains his concentration and can remain focused for the rest of the session or game.

RULE ADJUSTMENTS

Over the years, the ball has been modified to make it move quicker, and clip and swerve more easily. The back-pass rule has been introduced, and limited time in which the goalkeeper can keep the ball has been implemented. Are you sure you still want to be a goalkeeper?!

Over the last ten years, goalkeepers have become an additional fifth defender, with the back-pass rule and six-second rule put in place. Now the goalkeeper only needs to touch the ball and he is put under pressure. Defenders will use the back pass for safety and to take the pressure off themselves, so the keeper must be able to control, pass, head and even tackle with confidence in every situation.

On top of this, acting as the fifth defender means you must be able to read all situations early and act as a sweeper–keeper. For this, an air of caution must be adopted, as illegal challenges inside or just outside the eighteen-yard box are now red card offences. Therefore accurate timing and judgement

are required, especially in 1 v 1 situations – this is where a goalkeeper's football intelligence plays an important part in the game as he must read and anticipate situations which are about to unfold in front of him. Not only in defending, but also in attacking as the keeper is both the last line of defence and the first line of attack.

THE GOALKEEPER'S EQUIPMENT

Goalkeeping is such a specialist job that it is important that the correct tools are available to ply the trade. Goalkeepers are born with gloves on; long gone are the cotton green gloves for wet conditions and bare hands in dry. Clothing has also changed, with multiple colours available to keepers that may well be totally different from the team kit. Part of the goalkeeper's armour is the feel-good factor and if you look good, you will feel good. Remember the psychological attributes.

Boots

Check for wear and tear, and adjust the studs to suit the conditions of play, as one slip can result in disaster. Currently, most top keepers prefer the studded boots as opposed to the moulded ones, but again this is changing as the new blade type of boot has evolved to suit the lighter ball. The new traxion blades are also designed in stud form. The fact that they are available in a variety of colours is totally irrelevant, but the media will always scrutinize what the keeper is wearing and trends will be set.

Uniforms

Gone are the days of the plain green shirt – in now are the multicoloured tops with padded elbows and shoulders. Colours are brighter and bolder than ever before, which can have a psychological effect when forwards are

Equipment: Alan Blayney shows the match kit gloves and boots.

protection, especially around the knee area. These are excellent for training in, especially on hard surfaces, as they will help to protect you from injury and will also help to keep you warm in cold conditions, thereby also helping to keep muscles supple.

Gloves

Technology dictates that gloves change every season, as sportswear companies are modernizing them all the time. The gloves are the most important item for a goalkeeper, as the right gloves can help to improve the catching and handling of a ball. They can also be the most expensive item, depending on the type of foam used in the palm. You will need to maintain your gloves, as they will loose their effectiveness if not looked after. The gloves should be dampened prior to use for maximum catching potential and washed after use in warm water.

When choosing gloves find a pair that you feel comfortable with, whether they are roll-finger, flat-palm, fingertip or finger-save. Once you have made your selection, stick with it – why change what you are comfortable with? Remember, it's not the gloves that do the work, but the hands inside them.

Glove Bag, Cap and Towel

The bag is used to carry spare gloves and a sponge to keep the palms moist. The cap is an optional item, depending on the keeper's preference whether or not to wear one. However, a long-peaked cap is recommended to keep the glare of the sun from the eyes without impairing vision. But most importantly, a towel is essential, especially in the winter months, and the keeper should always carry one out with him. Just as the sponge is there to keep gloves moist, the towel is there to wipe the gloves in muddy conditions and to prevent them getting overly wet in bad weather conditions.

Always take good care of your gloves to maximize grip regardless of the conditions.

bearing down on the goal. The different shapes and colours can create the illusion that the keeper is bigger than he actually is.

The marketing of most premier clubs demands that the strip is fashionable and changes every season. Shorts tend to be in line with continental clubs – long to the knee and with padding to the hips to give additional protection. One of the traits amongst foreign keepers is to wear long bottoms in all weathers, which again are padded for extra

CHAPTER 3

The Warm-Up and Goalkeeping Positions

'Essential to gain maximum performance.'

The warm-up is without a doubt the most important aspect of goalkeeping, and preparing properly will help both the mind and body to achieve optimal performance. Extensive use of the ball is essential during the warm-up, as the goalkeeper should be comfortable and confident with the ball right from the start of the session.

The session should last at least 15 minutes and include light jogging, sideways movements, running and skipping, both forwards and backwards. Whilst skipping, you should incorporate some co-ordination work between the hands and feet.

ABOVE: Footwork.

BELOW: The warm-up.

By starting with this method of warm-up you will increase the body's cardiovascular system to an ideal heart rate of between 130 and 150 beats per minute, which will ensure an increase in body temperature. The muscles, tendons, ligaments and joint sites when stretched will then become more efficient in their working and will perform to their maximum potential, thereby reducing the chance of soft tissue injury.

Flexibility and stretching exercises are introduced when the body is warm, and will give a full range of movement for the goalkeeper. Ideally, you should include two stretching sessions in your routines; the first session should begin by holding stretch positions for at least 20 seconds for each movement. Do not jerk the movement, but keep an even and balanced position and hold to the point where you can feel the muscle tighten slightly. When working on the second session, push the muscles further and hold for the count of 30 seconds, then relax the position in a controlled and even manner.

Once you have completed the stretches, rotational mobility can be incorporated into the upper body. This is important for all goalkeepers as they mainly use their upper body, making it vital to stretch the arms, back and shoulders as well as the lower limbs.

Once the cardiovascular system is prepared and the stretching exercises completed in all areas required for the physical needs of a goalkeeper, then co-ordination work can begin. A few of these hand-and-eye co-ordination drills can be used to form ball familiarity before the handling and footwork exercises commence.

Perform these exercises individually:
• jog, pushing the ball from one hand to the other
• jog, bouncing the ball first with the right hand, then the left and finally together
• throw the ball above the head and catch with a one-footed take-off; practise with both feet

• push the ball in the air using only the fingers
• keep the ball in the air by punching the ball with a small jabbing action
• stand and throw the ball behind your back to catch, then throw back and catch in front
• lie on your back and, lifting on to your shoulders and feet, pass the ball around your waist
• hold the ball in both hands to start, then make a sweeping action by bringing the ball one-handed over your shoulder, changing in front to the opposite hand; repeat backwards
• standing with feet shoulder width apart, pass the ball through your legs, making a figure of eight movement
• standing with feet shoulder width apart, throw the ball through your legs and catch behind the head as the ball comes over
• hold the ball in your left hand, spin to the right and make a collapsing save on the ball as it hits the ground
• bouncing two balls with both hands, change the balls in front of your eyeline
• roll the ball through the legs with two hands, turn and repeat the process without the ball stopping. The ball should roll between 3-4 yards, with the keeper jogging to the ball once turned
• lie on the floor on your stomach, then bounce the ball with two hands and try to catch it before it bounces again
• do alternate toe-touching with the ball, changing hands by the feet.

THE WARM-UP – IN PAIRS

The following warm-up section concentrates on working in pairs, and involves additional work for the keepers in relation to distribution and footwork. These practices can be implemented in 10×10yd square boxes (see diagram). Only use a selection of these drills in your warm-up, not all of them.

Drill 1

1. Goalkeepers stand in opposite corners of the box with a ball each. They roll the balls to their right for the other keeper to move laterally (skip) and collect. Also repeat from the left. Ten repetitions.

2. The keepers pass the balls around their waists and underarm throw to each other. Fifteen to twenty reps.

3. Keepers stand back to back, passing a ball over the head and back through the legs. Twenty reps.

4. Keepers stand in the box facing each other, passing the ball with their feet. Each has compulsory three touches, then two touches and then down to one touch passing. Twenty reps each set.

5. Each keeper has a ball; one rolls the ball along the ground while the other throws the ball in the air, both working high and low balls. Twenty reps.

6. Both keepers have a ball each, standing 2yd apart. The keepers exchange the balls by throwing them two-handed and making a catch. This process requires quick hands and feet to catch and return. Twenty reps.

7. Keepers stand 10yd apart, and practise volleying and half-volleying to each other. Twenty reps.

8. One keeper holds a ball in each hand. The other keeper is positioned opposite him and must wait until one of the balls is dropped, then try to catch it before it hits the ground. Ten reps.

9. Both keepers stand 10yd apart opposite each other, each having a ball. The balls are thrown above the other's head height for a catch. Ten reps.

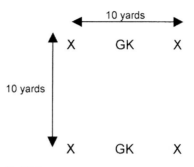

Drill 1.

10. One keeper has the ball and serves to the other by way of a throw, the second keeper must side-foot volley the ball back. Service can be front-on volley, side-foot volley or half-volley. One keeper works on handling, the other on the back-pass/touch. Ten reps.

11. Keepers stand 3yd apart. The keeper with the ball throws to the other, who must chest the ball either side of the keeper for him to catch. This can be by scooping up the ball or by a diving save. Ten reps.

12. One keeper passes a ball around his waist, while the other keeper serves him balls to be headed back. Ten reps.

13. Keepers stand 10yd apart, one keeper does a forward roll, and as he is getting to his feet the other keeper volleys the ball at him to make the save. Ten reps.

14. One keeper sits on the floor facing the other. The other keeper who is standing must volley the ball for the seated keeper to catch. Ten to fifteen reps.

15. Four balls replace the four markers and are placed 6yd apart. Keepers stand facing each other. One keeper moves to touch a ball either to his left or

right, while the other keeper copies his movements as a mirror image and must keep up with him. After 30 seconds, rest for 1 minute, and change lead keeper.

16. As no.15, but now use a diving save which requires the correct foot movement and technique. This time, the lead keeper must try to trick the other keeper into moving in the wrong direction. Rest and repeat as above.

17. Two keepers sit opposite each other. One keeper throws the ball to the side of the other for him to catch and return diagonally back to the other keeper. This exercise can be carried out at speed to improve handling technique (see the photo on page 89).

18. Use two balls; six or more keepers jog around the eighteen-yard box. One ball is used for throwing between themselves, while the other is used for passing. This exercise requires good hand-and-eye coordination.

19. As no. 18, but now the ball can be volleyed or half-volleyed between the keepers, while the other ball is still passed along the floor. The keepers should be limited to two touches.

STRETCHING EXERCISES

These stretching exercises are for goalkeepers of any age, as part of their preparation and to reduce the chance of injury.

Lower Limbs

Groins: While sitting, bring the soles of both feet together and ease both knees down and hold.

The groin stretch.

Hips/Flexors: With one knee bent and the other on the ground, push into the knee, keeping hips down. The stretch is felt in the top of the thigh. Change legs and repeat.

Stretching the hip flexors.

Hamstrings: Keeping the right leg straight, take one step back with the left leg. Bending the left leg slightly, take hold of the right foot with the right hand. The stretch will be felt at the back of the right leg between the knee and buttocks. Change legs and repeat.

Hamstring stretch.

Gluteus (Buttocks): While on the floor, keep one leg straight and place the other leg bent over the straight leg, then lean across and place the opposite elbow on the knee of the bent leg and pull it across the body. Change legs and repeat.

Michael Poke stretching the calves.

Gareth Williams demonstrates the gluteus.

Achilles Tendon: Stand with both legs bent, one in front of the other. Move the weight on to the back leg by bending both knees and pushing the weight down into the heel of the foot. Change legs and repeat.

Calves: Standing with one foot in front of the other, bend the front leg and keep the back leg straight. Weight is transferred down through the heel to the ground; push down on the back leg. The stretch is felt in the calf. Change legs and repeat.

Quadriceps: Stand on the right leg, take hold of the left ankle with the left hand and pull the foot up to the buttocks, keeping the knees together. The stretch will be felt in the front of the leg between the knee and the hip. Change legs and repeat.

Achilles tendon stretch.

The quadriceps stretch.

Upper Limbs

Shoulder: Take the left arm and place it over the head with fingers placed at the top of the back. Take the right arm and holding the left elbow gently pull towards the head. The stretch is felt at the back of the arm and shoulder blade. Change arms and repeat.

Upper body preparation is paramount, starting with the shoulders.

Wrist/Forearm: With the right arm straight, take hold of the fingers with the left hand and gently ease the fingers backwards. The stretch is felt at the underside of the wrist and lower forearm. Change arms and repeat.

The wrist and forearm are stretched in preparation for catching the ball.

Trunk: With feet shoulders-width apart, raise the right arm and place it over the head and stretch the body sideways in the direction of the right hand. The stretch is felt along the right side of the trunk. Change arms and repeat.

Trunk stretch.

Back: Lie on the stomach with palms on the floor shoulder-width apart and gently ease the arms into a press-up position, keeping the pelvis and hips on the floor.

It is important to stretch the lower back, due to the keeper's bending, twisting and turning.

THE WARM-DOWN

After every session you must warm down properly in order to reduce your heart rate to a resting state. A proper warm-down will reduce muscle fatigue and stiffness the following day and will help the body to get rid of the lactic acid that forms in the muscles when they stop working. It is most important, once the game or training session has finished, to replenish your fluid intake. It is also advisable that warm clothing is put on before starting the warm-down session.

Whereas in the warm-up, you are preparing the body and mind to perform at their optimal levels, in the warm-down you are preparing the body and mind to regain their normal state.

A light run with gentle skipping movements will help to relax the leg muscles and should be followed by a series of stretching exercises. These should be the same as those used in the warm-up, but each stretch position should be held for a count of at least 30 seconds. Goalkeepers should always concentrate on the upper and lower limbs, with time spent on relaxing the lower back area.

The whole process for this type of warm-down should last for a maximum of 20 minutes.

Goalkeeping Positions

'Providing the optimal chance to make the save.'

The foundation of good goalkeeping is sound techniques and the ability to use them at the correct times during a game. This chapter covers the basics of handling and goes on to explain techniques appropriate to the keeper. First, however, the keeper must achieve the correct starting position to catch or receive the ball.

A goalkeeper's starting position will always be relevant to the position of the ball on the pitch, and the situation that is developing as the game is in motion. When implementing good practice for positioning, the coach must consider the quality of the goalkeepers he is working with. The coach must assess each keeper's ability to read both the game plan that is unfolding in front of him and his ability to learn from mistakes.

Taking up the correct goalkeeping position will give the keeper an optimal chance of making a save or dealing with situations that arise throughout a game. There are three main starting positions that will help to deal with these situations.

Goalkeeping Position One: Dealing with Shots

Key points:
• feet shoulder-width apart
• knees slightly bent to 60 degrees
• weight transferred to the balls of the feet
• elbows tucked into the waist
• hands waist height and shoulder-width apart
• hands making the shape of the ball
• head slightly forwards, fixed and firm.

Michael Poke seen in a set position to deal with shots.

Goalkeeping position one – scenario:

- as the shot approaches, the keeper widens his feet positioning
- hands prepare to catch the ball
- for a catch above waist level, the thumbs come together so that the hands make a 'W' formation, with the fingers spread wide and in front of the bodyline
- tucked-in elbows act as shock absorbers when catching a ball at speed
- for a catch below waist level, the hands lower and the little finger comes together to make an 'M' formation with the fingers spread wide, again in front of the bodyline with the elbows tucked in.

Goalkeeping Position Two: General Play

Key points:
- the left foot is placed forward of the right or vice versa, depending on the position of the ball
- body and hands remain the same as GK position one.

Goalkeeping position two – scenario:

- as the ball is played, the keeper must first quickly assess the position of play and the direction the ball has travelled on the pitch
- once assessed, he can move forwards, backwards or sideways, depending on his decision
- balance is essential at all times.

Goalkeeping Position Three: Low Stance

Key points:
- balanced and prepared to react in any direction
- knees bent at 45 degrees
- hand position slightly lower with palms open.

RIGHT: *The low stance will help you deal with 1 v 1 situations.*

LEFT: *This position relates to general play.*

Goalkeeping position three – scenario:

• used in 1 v 1 situations when the ball is played through and the keeper becomes closer to the ball. By attacking the ball from this stance, the keeper will be able to drop to either side quickly by diving across and forwards
• aim the stomach towards the ball; this will give the forward less room to lift the ball. This can enable the keeper to make two types of save – either a spreading save or a blocking save, where the ball hits some part of the keeper's body and clears the danger area. Assessing and timing are paramount when using this technique
• refer to the section on 'Rule Adjustments'.

Footwork and Balance

'The quicker the feet, the easier the save.'

Maintaining excellent balance is vital for goalkeepers at any level of football, and while the keeper is moving, his hands should always be in a good catching position. To achieve this, the keeper should be on the balls of his feet, which will help to transfer the body weight forwards whenever possible.

Balance and foot movement can also make saves look easy, as diving will have a risk of not always making barriers behind the hands. By leading with the head; the rest of the body will follow, so when moving to either the left or the right the step should be short and in line with the body, and carried out in a gliding motion with one foot moving slightly behind the attacking foot. The feet must not click together or cross when moving in this fashion, as this could lead to the goalkeeper taking off on the wrong foot, which would result in a lack of distance and an incorrect dive to make the save.

Alan Blayney demonstrates one of the many footwork drills that are used during training.

During training and games the goalkeeper will use three main types of movements. These are running, sideways glide and cross-legged running.

Running

In certain situations during a game the keeper may be required to sprint or run from his goal. However, if in difficulties running or sprinting must be a last resort.

Sideways Glide

The keeper's feet should move in a sideways motion across the ground, without the feet touching or the ankles clicking. Nor should the feet cross, as this would affect balance and the ability to take off to make the save or catch. Hands should always be waist height, with the fingers pointing forwards to meet the ball. The head should be fixed and firm.

Cross-Legged Run

The body should be in an open position, and the chest should face the ball, enabling the keeper to dive sideways. This movement helps the keeper move and change position at speed across the goal or around the area. This technique is a much quicker movement than the sideways glide.

These are essential to a goalkeeper, and will help develop good hand and foot co-ordination as all saves or catches will demand fast and accurate foot movement. For instance, you can make a diving save by adding footwork to attack a high ball by timing the flight of the ball and moving quickly. These drills can be implemented into daily training sessions to improve the keepers balance, tempo and rhythm.

Drill 2
1. Run over the poles.
2. Glide around the poles.
3. Run sideways, two feet in each gap between the poles.
4. Jog back when completed.

Drill 3
1. Glide around the discs, touching each one with the inside of your hand as you pass.
2. Run forwards into the disc and run backwards as you go around. Repeat until finished.

Footwork drills can also be used in the goal with combinations of the above drills and finishing with a strike from the coach.

Drill 4
Goalkeeper moves sideways over the first three discs, then runs over the next three discs before coming in the small goal where the keeper receives a volley from the coach.

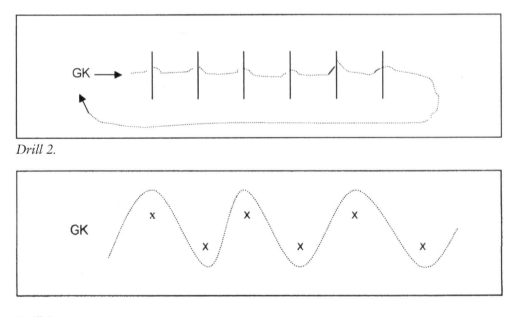

Drill 2.

Drill 3.

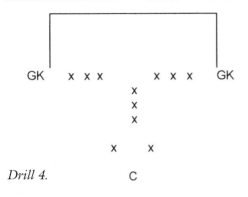

Drill 4.

Drill 5

Goalkeeper starts behind the top two poles. The coach calls left or right for the keeper to run over the first two poles, then sidesteps in the direction of the call and comes back over once both feet are placed the other side of the poles and steps into the goal for a volley served by the coach.

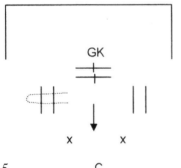

Drill 5.

Key Points for Footwork

Following are the key points for correct footwork:

1. Weight on the balls of the feet.
2. Short, sharp steps.
3. Feet should be shoulder-width apart (when gliding).
4. Knees bent.
5. Body weight forwards.
6. Hands in position.
7. Head fixed and firm.
8. When moving backwards, use small steps.
9. Balanced when stepping.

POSITIONING

'Making the goal look smaller makes the keeper look bigger.'

Goalkeepers who take up the correct position in relation to the ball will reduce the size of the goal, giving them the maximum opportunity in stopping a shot. Depending on distance and the angle, all keepers will tend to work at a distance of 4 yards from their line when shot-stopping. This will create an arc from post to post when the keeper is moving into and down the line.

The two elements of positioning are:
• moving into line
• moving down the line.

Moving into Line

If the ball is central to the goal, by moving into line the goalkeeper places himself to the middle of the ball. However, if the ball is in a wider position, then the goalkeeper's near post will become the priority. Because this area is more vulnerable, the goalkeeper will have a smaller near-post area to cover, leaving a larger far-post area. This gives the keeper one step to cover the near-post shot, and a step plus a dive to cover the far-post shot.

Moving Down the Line

After achieving the correct positioning into line with the ball, the next stage is to move down the line. This reduces the size of the goal for the forward to shoot at. The goalkeeper must make the correct decision as to when and where to stop when moving into the ball. Not moving far enough, and he will not cover the entire goal; moving too far and he becomes vulnerable to a chipped shot over him.

Making the goal look big.

Making the goal look small by stepping down the line.

Changing the goalkeeper's angle in relation to the position of the ball. In the second pictures, the keeper steps across and then down the line to reduce the goal-scoring opportunity.

Timing of the keeper's movement is also important – if the forward's head is down and looking at the ball or out of striking range, then the keeper will be able to move down the line. However, if the forward prepares to shoot, then the goalkeeper must get himself into a balanced set position ready to receive the shot. It is difficult for a keeper to make a save if he is slow moving into the shot, as a ball will always move quicker than the keeper can. It is also virtually impossible to dive sideways while still moving and unbalanced. The keeper must understand that every time the ball changes angle, then so must the keeper, in order to narrow the angle. Quick feet and balance are essential at all times when moving.

DEALING WITH ANGLED SHOTS

Drill 6

Four servers are positioned inside and outside the eighteen-yard box at various angles. The coach is positioned behind the goalkeeper and points to one of the servers, who takes a touch of the ball to the side of his cone and strikes at the keeper. The keeper who is facing the servers must wait for the touch from one of the servers before he can move into the shot. Six to eight reps.

Key points:
- move into line and down early and as quickly as possible
- get set into the goalkeeping position as the ball is struck
- always expect the strike
- use the correct catch or appropriate saving technique
- if parrying, play away from the danger area
- second saves must be dealt with.

Please note that this practice can also take place with the goalkeeper turning to face the coach for him to call the number of one of the servers. As the coach shouts the number, the keeper turns back into the appropriate server and deals with the strike.

Drill 7

Two markers are placed 4yd from the goal line. The goalkeeper moves down the line to receive a volley from S1, then glides across the line into S2 for a strike. This service is alternated between the two angled servers, and S1 volleys to begin the process. Six reps maximum.

Key points:
These are the same as above.

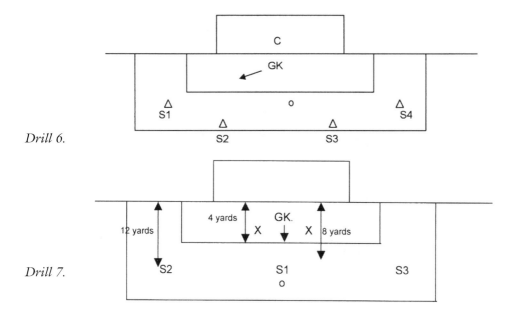

Drill 6.

Drill 7.

CHAPTER 4

Handling

'Safety and concentration are necessary to succeed.'

All goalkeepers require good handling skills, as they live and die by the quality of their hands. In handling skills practice sessions, the emphasis should be on the quality of service, as poor service will starve correct handling, resulting in fewer clean first touches.

A young goalkeeper's hands will not be as developed as an older keeper, therefore during games and training sessions the coach must always ensure that the correct size of ball is used for each age group. Lack of strength will also be evident, so good practice must be reinforced with lots of praise when clean catches are made.

We looked in the previous chapter at goalkeeping positions, which enable the goalkeeper to catch the ball correctly. Now we can move on to work on the catching shapes used when handling the ball at various heights throughout the game. There are nine main catching techniques to concentrate on when coaching keepers on how to deal with low shots.

DEALING WITH LOW SHOTS

1. The Long Barrier

As the ball approaches, the body must turn sideways into the ball, the knee of the leg kneeling meeting the ankle of the other leg. This forms a long barrier. The hands meet

The long barrier.

the ball in front of the bodyline with open palms and pointing fingers towards the ground. Always finish the catch by bringing the ball safely into the chest.

2. The Stoop

Glide into line as the ball approaches. Both feet must come together to form a barrier. The waist must bend and hands will be as in the long barrier, with eyes fixed on the ball. The ball is caught in front of the bodyline and safely gathered to the chest.

3. The Scoop

This technique is for dealing with the quicker shots that are bouncing into the goalkeeper. As the ball approaches, the keeper makes a small step forwards into the ball, keeping his eyes firmly on the ball.

The stoop.

The scoop: as the ball approaches, the keeper steps into the ball.

Hands must be prepared in front of the bodyline to help the momentum of collapsing. As the ball makes contact with the hands, the legs move slightly backwards and collapse at the same time.

With palms opened, the ball is safely gathered.

When gathering the ball into the chest, the body weight will move forwards and help to bring the ball in safely. It is very important to treat this type of catch with respect, as a lapse in concentration can be costly.

Touch with Feet

As the new law of dealing with back passes has been introduced, this means goalkeepers need to be comfortable with the ball at their feet as well as their hands. Position the body in line with the ball and place the side of the controlling foot in front of the body and hold feet firm to cushion the ball.

Touching with the feet is now seen as part of goalkeeping.

39

As the ball enters, make sure it is made safe.

The touch is very important, as it sets the keeper up to play the ball with his next strike.

As the ball is cushioned, at an angle of 45 degrees, it gives the keeper more chance of clearing the ball with his next touch, especially if a forward is closing him down.

5. Dealing with Shots to the Waist Area

Move into line with the ball, palms open as the ball approaches. Little fingers should meet together, making the 'M' shape.

Dealing with a shot into the waist.

Let the ball enter the waist and wrap hands around the back of the ball; the body weight must be forward and balanced.

6. Dealing with Balls at Chest Height – Front of the Chest

The ball is moving with pace. It can be caught in front of the bodyline, but the ball trajectory will need to be flat. Have the arms virtually straight and the elbows tucked in to act as shock absorbers and take the impact from the ball. Thumbs should meet, making a 'W' formation.

Catching in front of the chest.

Keep the head steady with eyes fixed on the ball as it approaches. Watch it right into your hands. This type of catch will allow the keeper to distribute early.

7. Dealing with Balls at Chest Height – Into the Chest

The ball will be approaching between waist and chest height, so the keeper's stance should be balanced with palms open. The chest must be relaxed on impact, and the ball should be accepted into the chest and cupped around the back of the ball.

8. Dealing with the Ball at Head Height

Position the body in line with the ball, with hands waist high, gliding upwards with thumbs making the 'W' formation. Arms should be raised to meet the ball early in front of the head, as this will help the keeper to see the ball enter his hands. The elbows must bend to act as shock absorbers and control the pace of the ball. Hands behind and to the sides of the ball with head fixed and firm behind the ball as a barrier.

ABOVE: Paul Jones, Wales Number One, takes a ball at head height.

RIGHT: Gareth Williams, Wales Under-19 goal-keeper, catches above the head at full stretch.

9. Dealing with the Ball above Head Height

This technique is the same as the previous catching shape, only the arms will become straight to give the keeper added reach to catch the ball in front of the head and eye-line. Tilt the head slightly backwards to see the ball into the hands. Sometimes a two-footed jump is required to give balance and a secondary barrier. At this point, the legs will also act as shock absorbers on landing.

Catching into the chest.

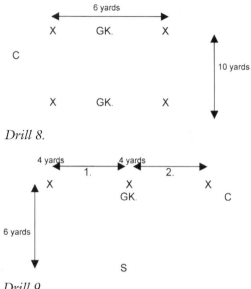

Drill 8.

Drill 9.

HANDLING DRILLS

When coaching the handling drills, please refer back to the handling techniques.

Drill 8
Both goalkeepers work each other using throws in one direction and kicking back to return. Work on all basic catching shapes and the back pass, both one and two touch.

Drill 9
Goalkeeper glides into goal 1 and picks up the ball from the server, then rolls to the server to strike first time into goal 2. On doing so, the goalkeeper should glide sideways to receive the next shot. Continue with a maximum of ten reps.

Drill 10
Both goalkeepers receive volleys from S1 and S2 and glide into the opposite goal to face another volley from the servers. Maximum of ten volleys to each keeper.

Drill 11
The goalkeepers are in a line behind each other. On the coach's command, they step into the cones and receive a throw, volley or side-foot into the goalkeeper. Once the keeper has dealt with the strike, he then moves smartly facing play out through the side cones. Movement into the ball can change coming through the cones sideways and service can be changed into diving saves.

Drill 12
The goalkeeper stands in the middle, in front of the markers. S1 volleys at the goalkeeper, who catches and returns the ball. Then reacts to S2, who strikes low for the keeper to save and moves into S3, who serves high for the keeper to save. Maximum of three reps.

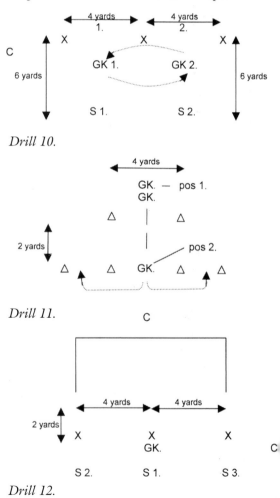

Drill 10.

Drill 11.

Drill 12.

Drill 13

The goalkeeper starts at S1 and works along the line of servers and back again, service is volleyed. For an advanced drill, the coach numbers the servers and calls a number at random for the keeper to react, or the markers are different colours and the coach now calls a colour for the keeper to react to.

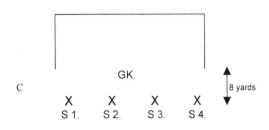

Drill 13.

Drill 14

The goalkeeper starts with the ball on his line. He rolls the ball out to the server for a strike first time. The keeper must move into the shot and adopt the correct position to make a save. The goalkeeper can also bounce the ball into the server for a volley or half-volley strike. The server can change the angle or distance of the shot. Maximum of eight reps.

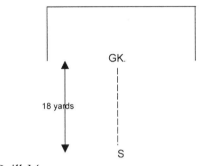

Drill 14.

Drill 15

A cone is placed a yard off-centre in the goal, the keeper stands a yard away from the cone and on the coach's call the keeper touches the cone. Whilst this is happening, S2 throws the ball to S1, who volleys the ball at the goal for the keeper to make the save or catch. S2 can also roll the ball to S1 for a side-footed shot. Eight reps working both sides.

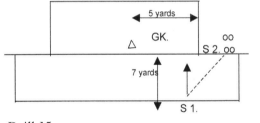

Drill 15.

SHOT-STOPPING
'THE REAL ART OF GOALKEEPING.'

All keepers find this the most stimulating and rewarding part of goalkeeping. Perfecting each different practice throughout the week will stand any keeper in good stead for the game. Making saves look easy and being in the right position at the right time will often win the game.

The coaching techniques practised during training sessions must be designed to be as close to match situations as possible. Unfortunately, at times outfield coaches can become too intense when working with keepers, and this will usually result in them being used for cannon-fire from outfield players. When this happens, the goalkeepers will get little or no rest and bad technique creeps into their session.

During game situations there is only ever one ball on the pitch at any one time – if the keeper makes a save, the game restarts when he distributes the ball. However, if the keeper parries or deflects the ball it remains in play and the keeper must take the appropriate action to deal with the next threat or danger.

Shots range from angled, dipped, long and close range, and swerved at various heights and speeds. Therefore, we must first look at the fundamentals of making diving saves, of which there are two standard methods, the diving save and the recovery save.

The Diving Save

Always use the leg nearest the ball when stepping into the save. Angle the foot so that the knee will go directly over the top of the foot. This will give you direction when diving to attack the ball.

Lead the dive with both hands and attack the ball as early as possible, diving across and forwards.

Try to aim your head behind the ball as much as possible, as this will create a second barrier and give momentum when springing off. The goalkeeper diving in an organized sequence should land in order of knee, hip, shoulder, and lastly should be the ball in a controlled manner. (Landing on the elbows will cause the ball to dislodge from the keeper's control). The keeper must watch the ball intently at all times until safely in his hands.

Once caught, the ball must be trapped with the leading hand behind the ball and the other hand on top of the ball. A keeper's weight should be forwards, giving him time to recover to his feet if required for a second save.

The ball may not always be held, so keeping your body open helps you to change direction if necessary. If not held, deflect or parry to the sides of the goal area, not back in the direction that the ball has come from. Use a stiff wrist and an open hand.

The Recovery Save

This type of save can be called upon when the keeper is dealing with a looping header or shot, and the ball has been chipped after the keeper has moved down the line for the shot. As the ball approaches, assess the flight and direction and turn the body sideways on. Foot movements should be either a skip motion backwards or even a crossed-leg glide, depending on the speed and trajectory of the ball.

Aim to get your body under the ball and take off from the foot nearest to your goal. Using the nearest arm to the ball, attempt to push the ball over the bar using an open palm with a strong wrist.

Eyes must be totally focused on the ball with a steady head whilst continuing to watch the ball as it goes beyond the bar.

All the techniques of shot-stopping are referred to in detail and explained so as to enable the coach to diagnose and correct drills if needed.

DIVING AND SHOT-STOPPING DRILLS

The coach holds the ball in one hand with the keeper standing 2 yards away. The keeper steps across with his right foot leading, dives across and forwards, leading with both hands, to attack the ball in front of the bodyline, taking the ball out of the coach's hand. The landing should be ankle, side of knee, hip, shoulder, then the elbow nearest to the ground in front of the body and finally the ball, which should be under total control. Six reps each side.

Drill 16

The goalkeeper starts by kneeling on the floor, the server side-foots the ball alternately left then right along the ground for the keeper to save. Coaches should pay attention to the shape of the keeper when diving (across and forwards). Body shape should be knee, hip and shoulder, with hands catching in front of the body. Six reps each side.

Paul Jones observing the ball going wide.

The diving save: hands, head and feet are important when making saves.

When diving, make sure you attack the ball across and forwards with hands leading.

LEFT: *The recovery save. Gareth Williams watches the ball going over the bar.*

ABOVE: *The diving drill.*

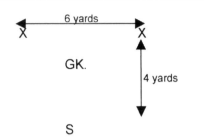

Drill 16.

Drill 17

The server plays the ball first to the left and then to the right for the keeper to save, the position of the keeper should be in a crouch shape in the middle of the goal. Principles are the same as for drill 16, with service being either high or low. Six reps each side.

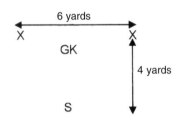

Drill 17.

Drill 18

On the coach's command, the goalkeeper, who is standing 1yd from the cone, touches it and turns into the coach, who serves the ball high for the keeper to move his feet and catch. Six reps each side.

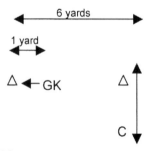

Drill 18.

Drill 19

A tyre is placed in the middle of the goal area, the goalkeeper is positioned with the left foot inside the tyre and the right foot facing the direction of the save. As the coach serves the ball, the keeper's weight should be on the right foot. He must then push up and out of the tyre using the right foot and catch the ball. This type of save is a power-step, where the keeper has no foot movement into the take-off.

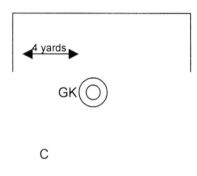

Drill 19.

Drill 20

Two poles are placed 3yd into the goal area, 1yd apart. The goalkeeper stands at the side of the poles and on the coaches call the keeper side steps the poles and makes a flying save across the goal. Six reps each side.

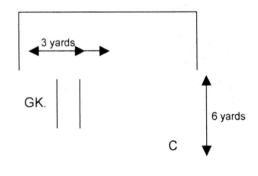

Drill 20.

Drill 21

The goalkeeper starts 2yd from his line, stepping down the line, through the discs and receives a strike from S1. Once the ball has been caught, he then moves into S2 and receives a low save, a throw or a volley. He repeats the scenario and move into S3.

Drill 23

Two goalkeepers are positioned in each goal, each having a supply of balls. The keepers can volley, throw, half-volley or strike at each other. If one of the keepers misses the target, he must run as quick as possible and touch one of the cones at the side of the goal. In the meantime, the other keeper can still try to score. This is an excellent session for practising all types of saves at speed. This drill is known as 'Goalkeeper Wars'.

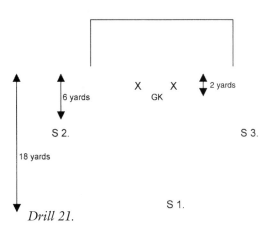

Drill 21.

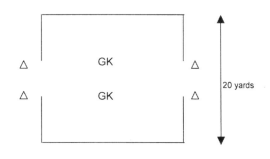

Drill 23.

Drill 22

On the goalkeeper's movement down the line, S1 strikes a dipping volley between the post and cone. The ball must bounce, forcing the keeper to make the appropriate save. Repeat the same service from S2 in order to work left and right of the goal. Eight to ten reps.

RECOVERY SAVE DRILLS

Drill 24

A cone is placed on the six-yard line, the goalkeeper runs out to the cone and touches it. As he does the server either throws or volleys the ball over the keeper to either catch or deflect it over the bar. Six reps maximum.

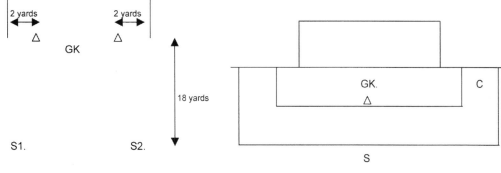

Drill 22.

Drill 24.

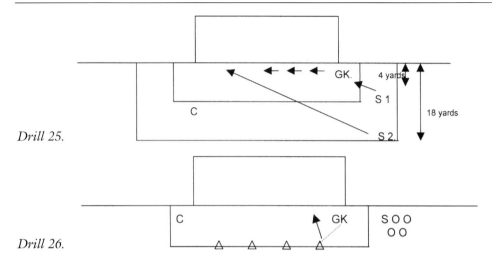

Drill 25.

Drill 26.

Drill 25

S1 volleys for the goalkeeper to catch as the ball is returned to S1. S2 volleys or throws the ball with a looping action. The keeper must recover the ball across the goal, and either catch or deflect it to safety. Repeat from left and right of the goal. Six reps maximum.

Drill 26

Four cones are placed on the six-yard line. On the coach's command, the goalkeeper runs to knock the cones over. As he does so, the server throws the ball above the crossbar for the keeper to deflect. Repeat from both left and right. Four reps.

DEALING WITH 1 V 1 SITUATIONS

'Transfer the pressure to win.'

When 1 v 1 confrontations happen in a game, most people think that the keeper has no chance, but this is not the case. This type of save can certainly be a turning point in a game. The goalkeeper is expected to be beaten, so where is the pressure – on the attacker who is expected to score, or the goalkeeper who is expected to make the save?

For the goalkeeper, winning a 1 v 1 situation can be the equivalent feeling of scoring a goal. Being brave and assessing situations early will help the keeper to make the correct decision; using the right technique will help to produce a positive result. To achieve excellent results the keeper must transfer the pressure on to the attacker by making his task more difficult. Standing big and forcing the attacker away from the goal will also gain a little time to help the defenders to recover and track back to assist the keeper in his dual.

When dealing with 1 v 1 situations the goalkeeper must work in three main stages.

These stages are:
• assessing the situation
• decision-making
• correct technique.

Assessing the Situation

The goalkeeper must assess the situation – whether he will be able to collect the ball early, or whether by using the correct action he can deal with the attacker controlling the ball. The keeper will have to consider three different scenarios that may develop during play.

Scenarios

a. The long ball – played into the space behind the keeper's defence.
b. Ball at attacker's feet – player dribbles through keeper's defence.
c. A rebounding ball – a shot is deflected into the path of an attacker positioned near the goal.

Decision-Making

This can only be based on the attacker's angle of approach, as he may be clear of the defence and the keeper will be required to make an instant decision and use an appropriate plan of action to deal with the situation.

Scenarios

a. The long ball – based on the distance between the goalkeeper and the ball. Can he win the race to the ball before the attacker, or will he need to dive at the forward's feet?

b. Attacker dribbles – the goalkeeper must assess whether the forward's touch is too far in front of him and he is likely to lose control, in which case he must act quickly to smother the danger or make a block.
c. Rebounding ball – if a ball rebounds to an attacker in a goal-scoring position, the keeper will have little time to think and will need to react early to rush the attacker and make a block or a spreading save.

Correct Technique

After assessment and positive decision-making to deal with these situations, the keeper must also be competent in carrying out the correct technique to suit each scenario.

The 1 v 1 situation.

Scenarios

a. The long ball – if the ball is outside the area, the keeper may be able to clear his line with a pass to one of his defenders, or by giving them the correct information to deal with the situation. If an attacker is chasing down the keeper, he may choose to clear long, or if the ball runs into the box he may have to dive at the forward's feet. The keeper attacks the ball with one hand behind the ball, with the other on top to trap and secure it. Also, aiming the chest at the ball gives an attacker nowhere to lift it if he has played the ball just before the keeper gets to it. By attacking the ball with both hands, a wider barrier can be created and used to block the ball. Using the legs can help the keeper to create a second barrier, which is an added advantage in spreading saves. It is important not to lead with the feet, as this creates a narrow barrier and shows more of the goal to the attacker.

b. Attacker dribbles – the goalkeeper must progress slowly in stages, narrowing the angle and forcing the attacker away from the goal. He must stay on his feet and transfer the pressure on to the forward either to shoot early, or to try to go around him to make the shot.

c. Rebounding ball – the goalkeeper must move quickly and instinctively, presenting his body as a big barrier. A panicked forward may miscue his shot.

In all situations, the keeper's starting position in relation to the ball will help to assess what action should be taken. Being positive and brave enough to use the technique with determination means less chance of injury to the keeper. The keeper needs to be totally focused mentally and aggressive in his approach, determined not to be defeated – by making himself look big, the goalkeeper will hopefully

panic the attackers and they may lose concentration, thereby increasing the keeper's chance to claim the ball.

The goalkeeper must be aware that timing and judgement are important, as fouling can result in a penalty kick being awarded and the keeper sent off. So the reading of every detail of play as it unfolds must be perfect, as well as executing the appropriate technique to make a save.

The technique for dealing with 1 v 1 situations is explained in detail in the section on Goalkeeping Positions, therefore when coaching see Goalkeeping Position Three: Low Stance to identify and diagnose the practice.

DRILLS FOR 1 V 1 SITUATIONS

Drill 27

The server runs with the ball to the left and right sides of the keeper, while the keeper practises his technique of diving at the server's feet. The server should let the keeper win the ball to start with as this will build confidence. Eight to ten reps in total.

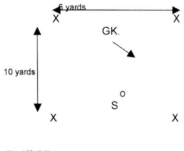

Drill 27.

Drill 28

Goalkeeper 1 starts with the ball and tries to dribble the ball around goalkeeper 2. If he succeeds he must place the ball on the goal line, between the two markers.

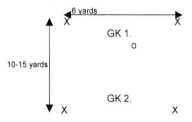

Drill 28.

Drill 29

Server plays a ball to an attacker, who plays a one/two and the server plays a through ball for the attacker to try a 1 v 1 situation with the keeper. Various services can be angled, and under or over hit through balls. Six reps maximum.

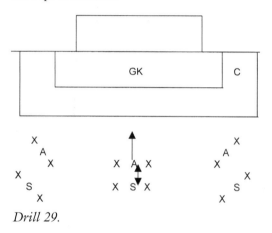

Drill 29.

Drill 30

Set up the same as drill 29, except that the server becomes a recovering defender. Once

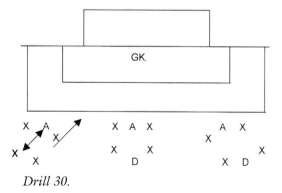

Drill 30.

the ball is played through, the defender must try to help the goalkeeper as quickly as he can.

Drill 31

The coach plays a through ball into the box for S1 to strike the ball first time. As the server starts his run into the ball, the goalkeeper must react and come to meet the ball to make a spreading save or block. This is a very demanding exercise, so keep to a maximum of six reps.

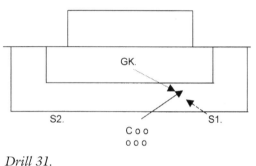

Drill 31.

DEALING WITH THE UNPREDICTABLE SHOT

In previous sections of this book we have looked at dealing with shots from angles and central positioning in relation to strikes on goal, and also the possible 1 v 1 situations. This section is dedicated to dealing with the unexpected – which is very real in the world of the goalkeeper every time he steps out on to the field.

Imagine your vision being blocked by your teammates and the opposition attackers – you might be able to make an easy catch, and one slight deflection can turn a basic save into a winning one, a save that will be based on pure reaction and instinct.

My days at the training ground are spent on creating the unpredictable. The next step will be to coach the goalkeepers to be able to deal with these situations and prepare them to be both physically and mentally ready for them when they arise during a game.

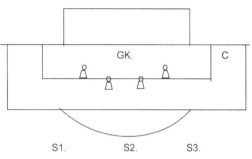

Drill 32.

Drill 33
The goalkeeper starts by facing the servers. He then turns to the coach, who calls the number 1, 2 or 3. The keeper then turns back into the servers to face a strike from one of them. If he parries the ball he may be required to make a second save. Eight to ten reps.

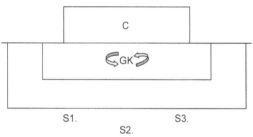

Drill 33.

Michael Poke responds to a deflected shot – to every action there must be a reaction.

Technique will often waver in the sessions when dealing with the unpredictable, so plenty of praise is required even when the keeper makes a save in an unorthodox style. So as long as the ball stays out of the net it will be classed as a save.

Drill 32
Four manikins are placed in front of the goalkeeper. S1 can either volley, half-volley or drive the ball at the keeper, who must make the save. If the ball hits the manikin the keeper's decision must be whether or not to gather the ball by dealing with either the rebound or second ball. The two other servers then repeat the process. Eight to ten reps.

Drill 34
The goalkeeper takes up a position on the angle ready to receive a shot from S1. As he saves, he makes his way across the goal ready to face a strike from S2. This is repeated from S3 and back into S2. Six reps maximum.

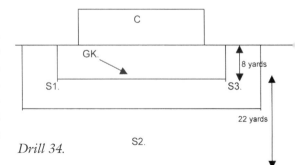

Drill 34.

Drill 35

The goalkeeper stands sideways on and as he turns to face play, S1 plays a low shot for the keeper to react to. Once saved, the keeper gets to his feet and moves across to receive a throw to the top corner from S2. After six reps change sides and repeat.

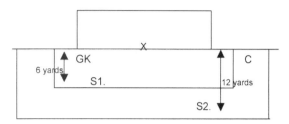

Antti Niemi demonstrates clean handling in Southampton's cup tie against Wolves, at St Mary's stadium.

Drill 35.

CHAPTER 5

Dealing with Crosses

'Defuse the potential by accepting the pressure.'

Dealing with crosses is regarded as the most difficult aspect of goalkeeping, as it requires quick decision-making combined with good technique when under pressure from the opposition. Therefore the keeper must work

Antti Niemi under pressure – he catches with ease.

hand in hand with the defenders as a single unit when dealing with the crossed ball. Not all balls delivered into the six-yard box are the goalkeeper's – with balls being made lighter and quicker, the defenders may be in a stronger position than the keeper to deal with certain situations.

Obviously, crosses into the penalty area are a potential source of scoring, so it is paramount that the keeper is competent in dealing with all types of situations. A hesitant goalkeeper will unsettle defenders, whereas one who can deal with crosses will take pressure off the defenders and give them confidence. When dealing with each potential goal-scoring cross there are some basic principles to remember so as to be able to counteract each situation.

Principles to remember:
• starting position
• position in relation to the ball
• assessing the flight
• decision-making and technique
• early information.

Starting Position

The starting position should be an open stance, with a 45-degree body angle and feet shoulder-width apart. The keeper should be balancing on the balls of the feet.

Feet should be moving in a bouncing action in anticipation of moving early and at speed, either forwards, backwards or sideways. If the ball is approaching from the

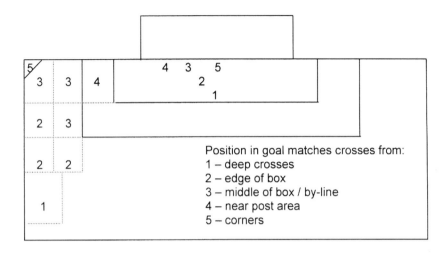

Position in goal matches crosses from:
1 – deep crosses
2 – edge of box
3 – middle of box / by-line
4 – near post area
5 – corners

Positioning in relation to the ball for crosses.

keeper's left, then the left foot should be pointing towards the ball and the right foot pointing out to play. Vice versa on the opposite side of play.

Position in Relation to the Ball

The area from which the ball is played will relate to the keeper's positioning. The delivery of the cross may be an in-swinging, out-swinging, driven or chipped ball.

The diagram above indicates the goalkeeper's position from where the cross is being struck. Also the goalkeeper must take into account the striking foot of the player crossing the ball, that is, in-swinging or out-swing.

Assessing the Flight

Before attacking the ball, the goalkeeper must wait for the ball to be struck, then as early as possible assess the line that the ball is travelling, as well as its speed and trajectory. By assessing the ball's flight path early the keeper will be able to attack the ball at the highest point. See movement 1 on the diagram on page 56.

If the keeper waits and attacks the ball late he risks the chance of letting attackers move across him and outmanoeuvring him in order to score. See movement 2 on the diagram.

By choosing 'path 1', the keeper attacks the ball at the highest point. If he takes 'path 2', it may give an opportunity for an attacker to get across him to score, because by waiting for the ball the keeper is catching the ball on its way down.

The goalkeeper's starting position.

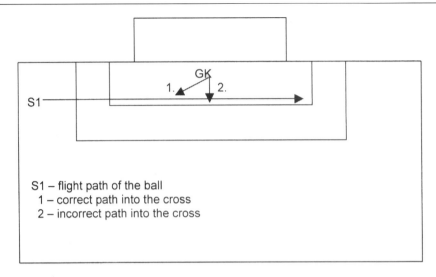

Diagram for assessing the ball's flight path.

Decision-Making and Technique

The goalkeeper must decide whether or not he can gather the cross or stay on his line and defend his goal. If he attacks the cross, he must decide early what path the ball is taking and not change his mind. The goalkeeper will have to move late, but attack the ball quickly to catch it at its highest point.

By delaying his movement, the keeper will gain valuable seconds in which to assess the trajectory of the ball, but will consequently have to move more quickly. Moving late, but attacking quicker, will enable the keeper to jump higher and gather the ball earlier.

Early Information

The keeper should and must communicate with his defenders before, during and after the ball has been crossed. The keeper must call early if he is going for the cross, giving his defenders time to react and cover the goal if it is left unguarded. If he is not going for the cross, the keeper must inform the defenders so that they can deal with the cross and avert the danger.

The two main calls from the keeper should be 'KEEPER'S' if he is going for the cross, and 'AWAY' if he is staying to defend the goal and leaving the ball for the defenders to clear. Confidence is the key when shouting and the keeper must be loud, clear and in control, as a late shout will cause confusion amongst the defenders. Please see chapter seven for communication.

CATCHING, PUNCHING AND DEFLECTING TECHNIQUES

Catching High Balls

Catching crosses involves jumping and catching the ball above the head. This technique is identical to that explained in the section Dealing with the Ball above Head Height, in Chapter 4.

Catching

Take off on one foot with the body weight going upwards and forwards to meet the ball. The non-take-off leg should be bent to give

Catching at the highest point. Timing and movement into the ball must be quick.

Using the arms gives the goalkeeper more momentum when attacking the ball.

protection and increase the spring. It is important that keepers practise taking off from both feet while using the other for protection.

Hands attack in an upwards motion through the bodyline and adds drive to attack the ball at the highest point, whereas outstretched arms will help to catch in front of the head and eyeline. The hands should be in the 'W' formation with the thumbs behind the ball, the head should be slightly backwards and eyes fixed firmly on the ball as it enters the hands.

Punching

The priority is always to catch the ball, but sometimes this may be difficult to achieve, therefore punching may be the next best option, either one or two-fisted. This technique is usually required when the ball is coming in amongst defenders and attackers and catching the ball is not an option.

When using two-fisted punches, target the bottom half of the ball with arms extended, as in a boxer's jabbing movement from the elbows. End with the arms extended, which will help to put height and distance into the ball and clear it from the danger area.

One-fisted punching is about timing and making sure the keeper gains good connection on the ball.

Two-fisted punching gives the goalkeeper a big area of contact on the ball.

One fist is used to punch the ball across the flight path, again using the jabbing motion, extending the arm from the elbow and finishing with arm extended to gain height and distance on the ball.

Deflecting

This technique is mainly used when the ball is played into the back-post area, travelling at speed and too high to catch, and when the goalkeeper is moving backwards without being able to see what is behind him. The keeper may choose to deflect the ball over the crossbar or deflect the ball away from the danger area if there are oncoming forwards.

The body must be sideways on to the ball and eyes should be fixed watching the ball into the palms, keeping wrists firm ready to make the connection. Put the ball into a safe area by directing it back into the area from which it travelled.

NEAR-POST CROSSES

If an attacker is in a goal-line position, the goalkeeper must position himself in the near-post area, as the attacker may play the ball back across the keeper's six-yard line. Therefore, by taking up a near-post position the keeper will be able to do one of two things – dive out and intercept the ball or defend the goal if the cross is a gamble that the keeper is unable to catch or deflect.

The goalkeeper should stand his ground and not anticipate or dive too early, but in doing so he must assess the cross and decide whether he is able to catch or deflect the ball to safety. Goalkeepers who leave their near post often make the goal bigger – if the ball was to be cut back, it would then be more difficult to defend the goal or make the save. The keeper may also lose his positioning and end up falling backwards as the cross approaches.

The cross itself could be either waist height, chipped far or into the middle of the goal, or even driven or passed along the

On deflecting, make sure you gain height and distance.

ground. Whatever the cross, the goalkeeper must be positive that he can deal with it; if not, it will be necessary to work along the goal line and make a recovery save.

When coaching these practices, please refer to the techniques on Dealing with Crosses.

Drill 36

Two goalkeepers stand slightly off-centre, opposite each other, each having a ball. On the coach's call, both keepers simultaneously throw the ball two-handed into the air, and catch the opposite ball. On landing, they change places and wait for the next call from the coach.

Drill 37

Two goals are placed 12yd apart and two goalkeepers stand on the far post with the coach positioned on the front post 6yd away. The coach serves the ball in-between the two keepers, who both attack the ball and compete to catch it. The keepers then change posts and compete again, working from both left and right posts. The challenge is first to catch three out of five.

Drill 38

The coach stands in the centre, 10yd from the goal. Two cones are placed on the six-yard box, level with each post. On the coach's throw, a goalkeeper moves into the ball and catches it at the highest point, then returns it back to the coach. The coach then serves to the next keeper from the opposite side. This service is repeated until each keeper has received four crosses from each side.

Drill 39

On the goalkeeper's movement around the cone, the coach serves an overarm throw into the far-post area for the keeper to attack and catch. The keeper catches the ball and throws it back to the coach, ready to serve to the next keeper, and returns to the back of the cue ready to repeat the service.

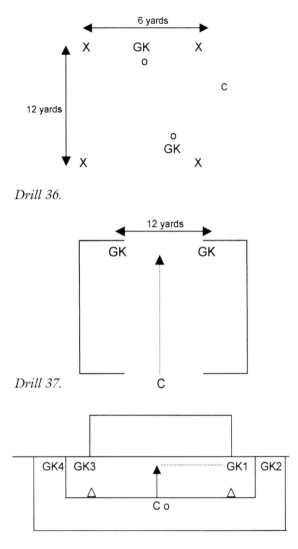

Drill 36.

Drill 37.

Drill 38.

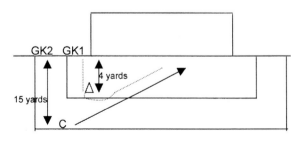

Drill 39.

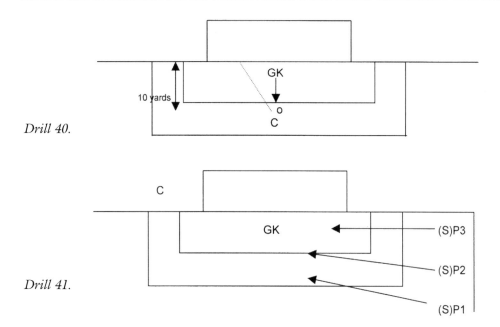

Drill 40.

Drill 41.

Drill 40

The coach stands in the centre of the goal, 10yd out from the line. The goalkeeper must run and touch the ball, which the coach is holding in front of him. On touching the ball, the coach serves the ball to either the left or right of the keeper, who must catch the ball whilst moving backwards. Eight reps, four each side.

Drill 41

The server crosses from position 1 for the goalkeeper to catch; service can be high, low, near or far. The server changes his position to P2 and P3 respectively, and therefore the keeper must adopt a fresh starting position in relation to the server. Once the ball has been caught, the keeper must find the server with a throw. Use both left and right side of goal and repeat six to eight times from each position.

Drill 42

S3 half-volleys or volleys the ball at the goalkeeper, who makes a catch or save and distributes the ball with a throw to S1. S1 controls the ball and crosses for the keeper to catch. Once caught, the keeper distributes again to S2 to repeat the process. The keeper catches and throws back to S3. This is repeated four times to each server.

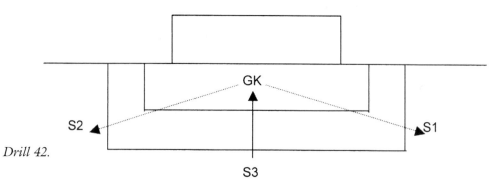

Drill 42.

Drill 43

GK1 starts with the ball. He throws it to S1, who controls the ball and moves it along the line, crossing for GK1, who is under pressure from the other keepers in the box. Once gathered, he must throw the ball out to S2, who repeats the process. The goalkeepers alternate after six crosses from each side.

Near-Post Cross

Drill 44

A1 plays the ball to D1, who in turn plays it into the eighteen-yard box towards the by-line. A1 chases the ball and decides to cross either low or high, chip or drive across the six-yard box. The goalkeeper must adopt the correct position for the cross and attempt to deal with the delivery. If he does not go for the cross he must stand and defend the goal. The servers should be changed so that they cross as in a match situation. Six reps each side.

Drill 45

This can be set up the same as drill 44, but when the server has made his move to the ball, A2 and D2 come into play as A2 makes a move to score. If the keeper does not go for the ball, then D2 becomes the recovery defender. Alternate both sides. Diagram is not shown.

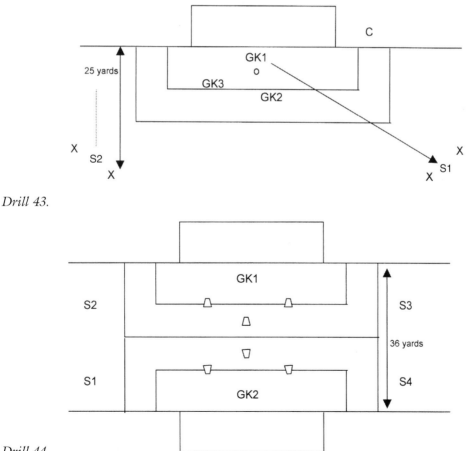

Drill 43.

Drill 44.

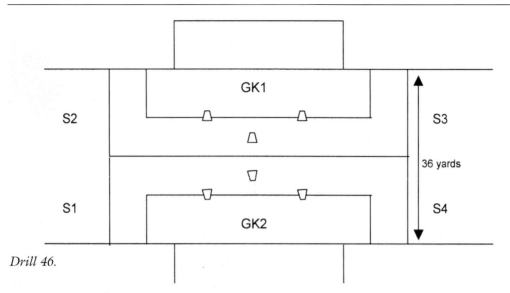

Drill 46.

Drill 46

Two goals are placed 36yd apart, with either six manikins or players in and around the keepers' six-yard boxes. GK2 starts by throwing or half-volleying the ball to GK1, who catches and distributes to S1.

S1 then controls and plays the ball to S2, who in turn takes a touch or strikes a cross for GK2 to catch, punch or deflect the shot whilst under pressure from attacking players. Once caught, GK2 distributes to S3, who plays the ball to S4 to cross for GK1. This is repeated so that each goalkeeper receives six crosses from each side. Service then changes so that the goalkeepers receive service from the opposite side. The servers should be mixed up so that the keepers receive in-swinging and out-swinging crosses. Manikins can also be used if outfield players are unavailable, as passive opposition for goalkeepers.

Deflecting Crosses

Drill 47

The goalkeeper positions himself 1yd from the goal line and the coach at the corner of the six-yard box. As the coach calls, the keeper runs to the cone and touches it; as he does so, the coach serves the ball towards the crossbar for the keep-

er to recover and turn the ball over the bar. This process is repeated four times. This practice can also be used for recovery saves.

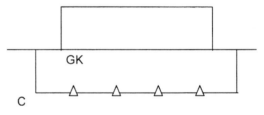

Drill 47.

Punching

Drill 48.

The coach stands 1yd from the goal line with the keeper positioned on the penalty spot. The goalkeeper jogs into the two cones placed on the six-yard line. As he

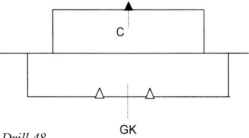

Drill 48.

approaches, the coach serves the ball above the crossbar. The keeper must attack the ball and punch it over the bar, with the coach jumping or trying to obstruct the goalkeeper from the ball. Six reps maximum.

Drill 49

GK1 sits in a 4yd goal while GK2 serves the ball for GK1 to punch both left and right-handed alternately over the top of him into GK3. Ten reps maximum each hand.

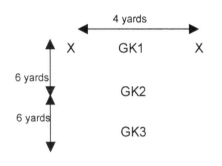

Drill 49.

Drill 50

GK1 kneels in the 4yd goal. GK2 serves the ball for GK1 to fall forward into, and using body weight punch it through two-handed into GK3. Ten reps maximum.

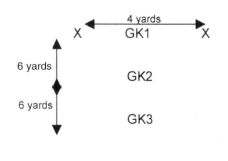

Drill 50.

The flying Finn makes a great save in a Premier League game versus West Ham United.

CHAPTER 6

Distribution

'Never leave anything to chance.'

Once the keeper is in control of the ball, there is nothing more frustrating than losing the ball through bad technique or lack of concentration or vision.

Distribution is an area where top-level goalkeepers are expected to keep possession of the ball when kicking or throwing. The new laws demand that goalkeepers are able to play with both feet and able to pass with accuracy, as well as knowing when and where to use the correct type of distribution. Nothing can be left to chance, so consistent practice of both kicking and throwing is para-

Paul Jones striking through the ball in a premier league game.

mount and will improve technique and help the team to break early, sending the defence into attacking positions when the correct distribution is used.

THROWING

There are four main techniques for throwing, each of which must give the player the opportunity to control the ball early. Throwing the ball will enable the team to gain possession in its own half, but remember that a thrown ball will never travel as far as a kicked ball.

Underarm Roll

The starting position must be with the back bent in a crouching position, with the back leg bent slightly and the front leg stepping into the direction of the target. The ball is released with an underarm bowling action. The underarm roll-out is used for short balls to the fullbacks, or into midfield when there is time and space to do so.

Javelin Throw

The ball is placed in the palm of the hand with the fingers placed behind the ball. The arm is raised and bent to the side of the head. As the arm is brought forward, the fingers push through the ball with the body in line with the intended target. The ball is released at the highest point, which helps to inject speed and create a quick, flat trajectory.

The under-arm roll.

Javelin throw.

Overarm Throw

The keeper's body must be in line with the direction that the throw is to travel, with the weight on the back foot. The other foot should also be pointing in the direction the ball is to travel. In a bowling action with a straight arm the ball is released at the highest point, and in doing so the weight now transfers to the front foot. The body weight must follow through to the ball from the keeper's feet, not his shoulders.

Discus Throw

This is an excellent technique for throwing great distances with a low trajectory. The ball should be held at arm's length and at shoulder height, with the body weight on the back foot. The weight will change to the front foot as the arm is brought around the side of the body and released just in front of the keeper's body.

Over-arm throw.

Discus throw.

THROWING

Drill 51

The goalkeepers throw the ball back and forth, practising each of the throwing techniques.

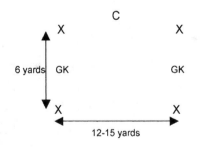

Drill 51.

Drill 52

Goalkeepers play piggy-in-the-middle with GK1, throwing the ball using any of the four techniques. He must try to throw past

GK3 who can dive, jump or knock the ball out of play by parrying or deflecting. GK1 and GK2 cannot drop the ball, and have 6 seconds to release the ball. If GK3 makes a save or if the ball is dropped, the keepers exchange places.

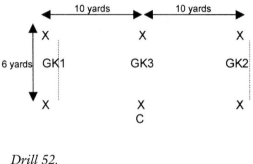

Drill 52.

Drill 53

GK1 is in a 6yd goal, with three other keepers placed 20yd away. GK2 and GK3 each have footballs and the object is to find the keeper without the ball, by throwing. Therefore GK2 throws to GK1, who must catch and throw to GK4. (You cannot throw backwards in the direction that the ball has come from.) This drill can also be used for one and two touch back passes. Ten reps maximum and change.

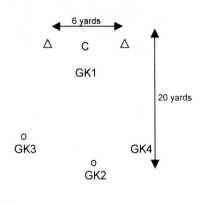

Drill 53.

KICKING

Goalkicks

When striking the ball, the top and inside of the foot are used. On approaching the ball, aim to connect with the bottom half of the ball with your non-kicking foot at a distance of approximately 9in to the side of the ball. This distance will help you to keep your balance and put extra force into the kick. The head should be steady, with the eyes fixed firmly on the ball. Aim to kick the ball between the fullbacks and the centre-half either side of the pitch.

Volley

Holding the ball at arm's length, drop it on to your kicking foot. Do not toss the ball into the air, as this will increase the chance of missing the connection. Your weight transfers forward into the ball, which ensures a solid strike through the ball. This kick causes difficulties for the defenders, as the ball travels a greater distance and with added height.

When finishing, make sure the foot follows through the ball.

Half-Volley

Timing is vital for this kick. Use the same technique as for the volley, but this kick involves the ball being bounced and then kicked, producing a low trajectory, which will gain speed and should be a much more accurate kick.

Striking through the ball.

The volley technique.

The half-volley.

Dribble and Drive

When the ball is caught by the keeper and his back four have pushed up, this kick can be used to gain extra penetration into the attacking third and will give the defenders some valuable breathing space whilst under pressure. The ball is thrown or played out of the area and kicked just as a goal kick. The ball should be struck when it is stationary and kicked into the channel areas. Do not let the attackers get close to the ball, as this can cause panic and result in mistimed strikes and a poor kick. Concentrate at all times and keep eyes firmly fixed on the ball.

THE BACK-PASS

This is without doubt the most important and difficult part of distribution. Safety in all situations is paramount, so don't gamble; after all, you are the last line of defence. Attempting to dribble around the opposition can lead to the keeper slipping or getting caught out of position, therefore if in doubt, boot it out. Let's be honest – no one is going to score from row Z.

Paul Jones seen here using the dribble and drive kick.

Antti Niemi dealing with a back-pass at Stamford Bridge.

All goalkeepers must be able to deal with moving and bouncing balls in a confident manner, and dealing with the back-pass in today's game is a major part of the goalkeeper's role. When clearing, the keeper's body should be between the ball and the goal if possible and observed right up to the clearance of the ball.

In each situation, the goalkeeper must adjust the angle and distance between himself and his defenders ready to receive the ball. He should try to play the ball high and wide of the goal.

Assessments have to be made about each back-pass, and judgements made on the following aspects:

- speed of the ball
- distance and angle between the ball, keeper, attacker and defender
- whether to play the ball with one or two touches.

Concentration is the main aspect when dealing with any ball passed back. Players use the back-pass to buy some time for the team, using it to get out of a difficult situation or to change the run of play and keep possession.

Composure and control will help the keeper to decide how many touches he will require to distribute the ball with complete accuracy. The defenders should also know the keeper's stronger foot when rolling the ball back to him. At the same time, judging the weight of the pass from the defender is paramount, giving the keeper one of two options, either a first-time strike or to control the ball and play with second touch.

Depending on the type of ball and trajectory, the keeper must be prepared to act with quick instincts in deciding where to play the ball. If two touches are required, the first should be out of the keeper's feet using side-foot control, which puts the keeper in a position to clear with his next strike.

If the keeper decides it is too dangerous to chance a second touch, he must clear the ball with height and distance. Some keepers will strike through the ball, while others will use the instep of the foot to help the ball forward; the latter means less chance of errors and increases the size of the area being struck to clear the ball.

The goalkeeper will sometimes be in a position to bring the ball forward if opponents do not close him down, and if he has the time and space he may choose to play in one of three ways – passing long, playing through to midfield or going wide to the fullbacks.

When a ball is played back by a defender it is important that the goalkeeper does not close down the space of the approaching player. The keeper should therefore create an angle so that the defender can play the ball to the keeper's favoured foot. Playing the ball in this way will give the keeper an excellent chance of clearing the ball with height and distance.

In the diagram below, the defender is playing the ball to the keeper in six ways. Position 1s show the angle of the pass to a right-footed keeper, whereas position 2s are for a left-footed keeper. Notice the angle and depth of the goalkeeper, which gives him time and space to play the ball.

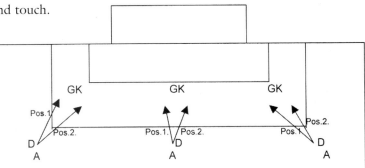

Creating angles for back-passes.

KICKING

Drill 54

GK1 plays the ball to GK2, who must have three compulsory touches, then plays the ball back to GK1, who repeats the sequence. This can be changed into the keeper having two touches and then into one-touch passing.

Drill 55

GK2 starts with the ball, and plays it into GK1, who controls the ball with his left foot, and takes it to his right side. He then plays the ball with his right foot to GK3, who in turn controls the ball and plays it back into GK2. GK2 returns it to GK3, who controls the ball with his left foot and plays the ball with his right foot to GK1. This drill can also progress into one-touch passing, with the goalkeeper in the centre putting the other keepers under pressure. Repeat the drill so that all goalkeepers have worked both the middle and sides, playing with left and right feet.

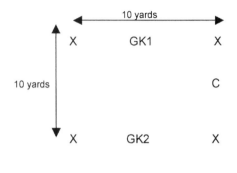

Drill 54.

Drill 56

The coach stands 30yd from the goal. He plays a through ball to GK1, who must decide whether to take a touch or to strike first time into either of his target goalkeepers. When the coach plays the ball, one of the attackers can go after the ball and cause the keeper to make a quick decision.

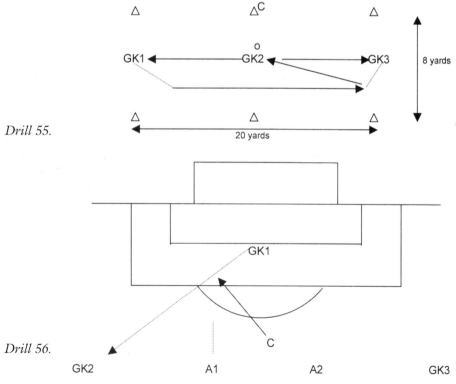

Drill 55.

Drill 56.

SUPPORTING DISTANCES

'Assess, decide and react.'

Supporting distances during the game are dictated by the position of the ball on the field of play. The position of the ball is a major factor as to which way the keeper supports the defenders. If his team is attacking, the keeper will have a big space to cover and this can ultimately allow him time to read and deal with various situations. However, if his team are defending the penalty area, the keeper is dealing with a smaller area and must adapt accordingly. This leaves him less time to make decisions and deal with situations that arise, making the margin for error much smaller – his decision has to be the correct one.

Goalkeepers are now an additional defender and are used to gain possession of the ball or as a passing option. From the keeper's position you have a perfect view of the build-up of play and the whole picture, and the keeper should communicate this information to the defenders at all times. Communicating the correct information to the defenders will help them to eliminate danger early.

The main factors and elements of supporting play are:
- goalkeeper's starting position – in relation to the ball
- goalkeeper's movement – balance and ability to adjust
- appropriate action – positive decisions and taking charge
- communication – clear information and variation of tone.

A goalkeeper's starting position should always be in relation to the ball at all levels of the play. If the ball is in the attacking third of the field, then the keeper

Antti Niemi supporting the defence.

should be on the front foot in case he needs to advance from the goal area at speed. Distances and angles of support must be reassessed during the game as the ball moves across the pitch. The defenders' and attackers' pace will frequently change, so the keeper must adjust to that too. Judgement of through balls or balls played into the space behind defenders is both an important and a difficult part of goalkeeping.

The keeper must assess and be prepared to deal with early dangers:
- the player in possession of the ball and how much pressure is being applied
- positions of the defenders and the attackers
- pace of the defenders and attackers (see diagrams for supporting role of the keeper).

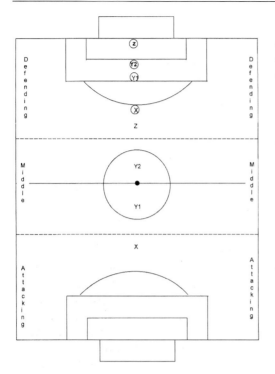

The diagram above shows the movement that the goalkeeper should adopt in relation to play during a game, which will be forwards, backwards and sideways depending on the position of play to best suit reaction times. The circled letters relate to the position of the goalkeeper, whereas the other letters relate to the position of the ball.

USE OF THE SWEEPER-KEEPER

In conjunction with supporting distances, the goalkeeper must be able to sweep up any through balls, as teams these days will try to play a high line when defending. This pressurizes opposing teams, but tends to create a gap between the rearmost defender and the keeper. Adjustment between the two is important so as to prevent an open space for a long ball to be played into, and the keeper must constantly examine the angle and distances while play is in motion.

Practice of through balls is a vital part of a goalkeeper's weekly training routine. There are several factors to be considered when dealing with through balls.

These key factors are:

1. The through ball, speed and distance of defenders in line with the attackers.
2. Can the goalkeeper gather the through ball by backing off in his area if the ball is over-hit?
3. Can the goalkeeper clear the ball if it is under-hit and an attacker may get to the ball before a defender? If so, the keeper must be positive and clear his line with height and distance.
4. Can the goalkeeper drop off and create an angle for a back pass if the defender is able to get to the ball before the attacker? The goalkeeper must always ensure that he doesn't close down a defender's space, leaving a tight area to play the ball back into. See diagram on page 69.
5. Can the goalkeeper regain ground if the attacker is in possession of the ball in order to make a save or buy time for his defender to make a tackle?

DRILLS FOR SUPPORTING DEFENCE PLAY

Drill 57

The middle server starts with the ball, and can play the ball sideways to either S1 or S2, who must run on to the ball. As the middle server plays the ball into S1 he calls 'back pass or through ball' and the keeper must deal with either scenario.

If he plays a back pass, the opposite server from where the ball is played goes wide to act as an out ball if the keeper has time; if not he must clear his lines.

If he calls a through ball, the ball must be over-hit and followed by S1. The goalkeeper must now attack the ball to make a spreading save.

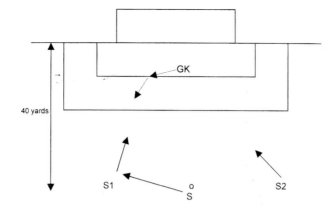

Drill 57.

Coaching points:
• starting position
• movement once the ball is played
• speed from line (if over-hit)
• spreading save or pick-up
• if back pass – decision, first time or two touch
• time to play to opposite fullback (supporting angle)
• clearance – height and distance
• communication – keepers

Progression

Phase of play 7 v 7, 60yd long and the width of the pitch. Target areas are placed the other side of the halfway line for the defending team to attack.

Drill 58
• Area is 70×50yd.
• Balls are placed around the area
• Offside rules in attacking third/normal restarts

Game begins with GK1 who half-volleys or throws into GK2 and he can distribute into one of his team (the 'B's).

Coaching points
• starting position of the goalkeeper in relation to the ball in all thirds of the game
• body position, for example whether the keeper is on the front foot and able to move quickly from his goal if a ball is played beyond the defenders
• positioning of the defenders; compactness
• pace of both the defenders and attackers, for example whether the defenders need to drop deeper and the keeper needs to adjust his position accordingly.
• communication needs to be loud, clear and concise and the tone should vary
• decision-making – the keeper needs to be positive in dealing with situations that arise
• distribution – dealing with back passes; technique when kicking, and one or two touch.

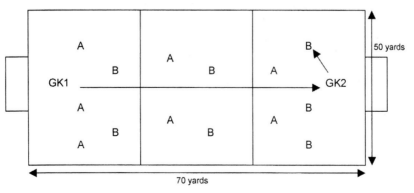

Drill 58.

CHAPTER 7

Communication and Defence

'The art of correct information.'

Communication is a vital tool for goalkeepers, as they can see the whole picture while the game is in motion. It is essential that goalkeepers organise and give information to defenders, especially in set-piece situations.

The guidelines for communication are as follows:
- WHAT – instructions that are specific to each situation
- WHEN – early directional information
- HOW – loud, clear and dominant in tone.

Goalkeepers who talk will give confidence to defenders and help their teammates to react to situations that they may not always be aware of. Good early communication will enable players to counteract build-up play by getting into position early and dealing with the immediate danger.

Following are guidelines of what to say in each situation. They are aimed at helping defenders to react early whether or not they are in control of the ball.

When IN CONTROL of the ball:

1. Teammate has time with the ball. 'Time – Turn' – 'Time – Two Touch'.
2. Teammate is under pressure. 'Man-up' – 'Away man-on'.

3. Keeper wants the ball played back to him. 'Play it early' – 'Head it early' – 'Keeper's on'.
4. Keeper wants defender to leave the ball. 'Keeper's ball' – 'Let it run'.

Organisation is paramount at set plays. Paul Jones demonstrates.

When NOT IN CONTROL of the ball:

1. Pressure required on the ball. 'Get tight' – 'Close him early' – 'Stand up'.
2. The keeper must give guidelines when he wants the defence to hold the line. 'Hold penalty box/eighteen yards' – 'Six yards and hold' – 'Hold level with the ball'.
3. Ball has been cleared. 'Squeeze early' – (if the ball has travelled a long distance). 'Get up, hold' – (if the ball has travelled a short distance).
4. Make play predictable. 'Show him inside/outside'. 'Show him left/right.' 'Stand him up' – 'Don't let him turn'.

DEFENDING SET PLAYS

The common factor in goal scoring tends to be set plays and this section is dedicated to covering and helping to achieve the correct starting positions, including positions for the defenders to adopt to suit the situation. Giving away fewer free kicks, corners and throw-ins around the eighteen-yard box means less opportunity for your opponents to score.

The three hard-and-fast rules for dealing with set plays are:
• planning and organization
• collective responsibility
• concentration.

Organization of set pieces should always be rehearsed during training sessions, so that when situations arise during play the planning will be implemented and confusion avoided. Most managers will know how other teams tend to operate and give players instructions of what is required during attacking play.

The goalkeeper will become the main organizer during set plays and must concentrate not only on his job and the task ahead, but also on whether his teammates are focused on their roles. If a substitution takes place, the priority of the player entering the field is to carry out the task of the player he is replacing along with any instructions he may bring on to the field from the coach or manager.

Staying alert when a set play is in motion is vital for all defenders, and this is when a goalkeeper must dominate each situation in a controlled manner, enabling players to respond quickly. A goalkeeper who talks will influence the players around him and keep them on their toes. In today's modern game most premier league clubs have computerized systems installed so as to be able to analyse both defending and attacking set plays. Management teams will spend time watching and diagnosing the opposition's free kicks, corners and throws in preparation to advise their players of what to expect during certain situations.

CORNERS

Goalkeepers should be positioned in the middle of the goal, with an open stance of a 45-degree angle to the ball, and between a yard and yard and a half from the line. Keepers should be on the balls of their feet, ready to travel in any direction at speed. It is also important to communicate with defenders, making sure that they are marked-up and switched on to what is about to happen. (See diagram for set-up.)

Defending corners – points for consideration:
• club policy – man on man – zone marking
• out-swinging – in-swinging
• how many attacking players – short corner
• how many defenders to counteract
• roles of all players
• defenders – front and rear posts
• man-to-man marking – choice of players – height and best attackers of the ball
• zone – areas of organization – prioritize.

Corner set-up.

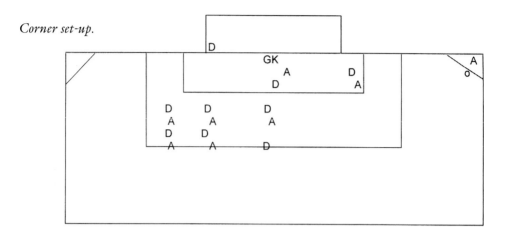

THROW-INS

Players are able to throw great distances and throws will often reach the danger areas. The position of the keeper should be the post to which the ball is being aimed. This may cause the thrower to go short, although if it is a long throw the keeper must get into a position where he is able to catch the ball. However, the problem for the keeper is that he will have a number of players around him and may not be able to make a clean save. In this situation defenders may be better equipped to deal with the ball. If the keeper goes for the ball, the safer option may be to punch the ball to safety. (See diagram below for set-ups.)

Defending short or long throws – points for consideration:
• distance from goal
• long or short throw
• history of player taking throws
• positioning of defenders to counteract attackers
• height factors – pair the best v best
• communication
• face play at all times – be alert
• when to hold – when to squeeze.

Defending a short throw.

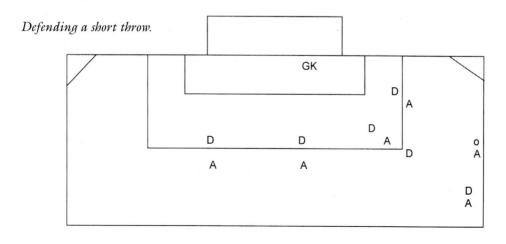

Defending a long throw.

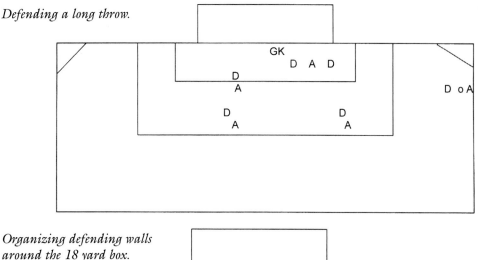

Organizing defending walls around the 18 yard box.

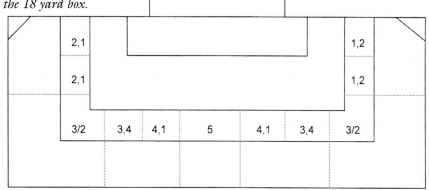

THE DEFENDING WALL

Organizing free-kick situations should be carried out early and with authority (see diagram above). Gaining a clear view of the ball is the aim of every goalkeeper, but it is vital not to over-cover one side of the goal as a result. Once the number of players in the wall has been identified, the keeper must make sure that the covering players are aware of all possible eventualities.

FREE KICKS

Organization is crucial when dealing with free kicks around the eighteen-yard box, and the goalkeeper must line his wall early and be able to see the ball clearly. Positioning himself on the end of the wall will give him the maximum opportunity to make a save, therefore being central to the goal area will give the keeper an equal chance to deal with any eventuality. If using someone to charge down the ball (four in the wall and one charging down the ball), the keeper must make sure that he positions himself between the last man and the charger (see diagram). The keeper must try to see the ball at all times, as being out of sight or out of position will give the attacker a chance to pick his spot.

Defending free kicks – points for consideration:
• early organization
• direction and information – loud, clear and concise

- history of the free-kick taker
- left or right-footed – in-swinging, out-swinging or driven
- indirect or direct free kick
- number of players in the wall – normal or split
- whether the goalkeeper or outfield player lines up the wall
- position of the tallest players
- whether the wall stands or jumps on strike
- whether a charger is needed, and his position in relation to the ball
- goalkeeper's starting position
- positioning of defenders away from the wall
- the role of the wall, defenders or charger if the ball is passed
- the wall players' recovery when the ball is struck
- the referee's decision – whether the free kick is moved forward
- early reorganization
- whether the wall lines up on the goal line, and the keeper acts with or without the players.

PENALTIES

Goalkeepers these days are allowed to move upper and lower limbs, which helps to put the penalty taker off, while at the same time making the goal area look smaller. The keeper will usually have a chance of saving the kick if he moves early; most penalties are saved because of this factor.

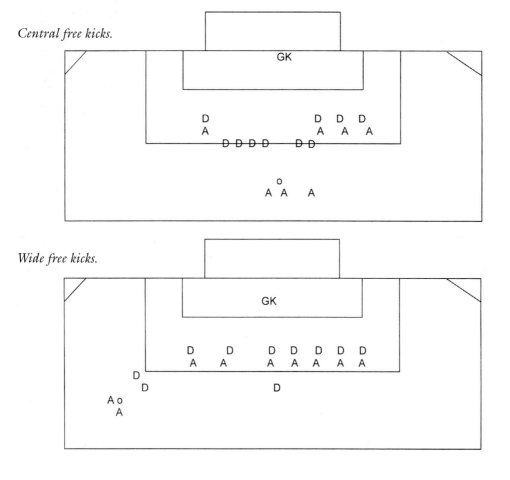

Central free kicks.

Wide free kicks.

When facing a penalty, the keeper must assess the striker's run-up, body position and angle of the striking foot on approach, as all of these factors will help the keeper to decide where the ball is going to go. Moving his arms and jumping from side to side can often distract the penalty taker, but at the same time the keeper must ensure that his feet are in contact with the ground at the point when the ball is struck. Some goalkeepers will tend to stand off-centre to the goal and again this can be off-putting, but the keeper must then step back into the larger area of the goal as the ball is struck to give himself the optimum chance of making the save.

Most strikers will hope that the keeper will not move before the ball is struck, as this will give the keeper a slower start and the attacker more chance of scoring. If the keeper has to block or parry the ball, he must ensure that he has gained sufficient distance from the goal and that his players around the eighteen-yard box are alert and prepared to deal with a rebound.

Whatever the keeper's tactics, any save from the penalty spot is an excellent save. This is a complete test of psychology and boldness for the keeper, as he must assess in which direction the penalty will go, knowing he is totally alone.

A low shot is well gathered by
Antti Niemi.

CHAPTER 8

Setting Phases of Play and Small-Sided Games

A mistake by a goalkeeper can cost a team the game. The saying 'you're only as good as your last game' applies to goalkeepers more than to any other player.

Coaching goalkeeping is not only about working with keepers in isolation and training them in functional aspects of the game, it is also about working with the back four as a unit and practising elements of real match situations. When working with any goalkeeper, there will come a time when the manager or coach will require the keeper to participate in other aspects of training with the rest of the team.

Time must be spent on how the team will play to cover the tactical issues of play and the keeper's role within the team. Certainly at the professional level this happens on a regular basis and the goalkeeping coach will be there to observe the keeper's positional, tactical and technical abilities whilst play is in progress and to assess the entire performance.

It is important for young keepers from an early age to practise game-based situations and appreciate the role of the goalkeeper in every situation of the game; after all, the most talked about part of goalkeeping is decision-making.

When organising small-sided games (SSG), phases of play or full-scale games, guidelines of what is required of the keeper and players must be specifically explained. When planning, coaches have a number of issues to consider.

Points to consider for small-sides games, phases of play or full-scale games.

- what is being coached – technical/topic
- coaching area and size in relation to the above
- selection and number of players – quality
- equipment – ball, bibs, footballs
- offside lines (SSG or 11 v 11)
- target areas (phase of play)
- rules and conditioning
- position in which to start
- coach's position
- demonstrations if needed.

Functional Practice

Functional practice is organized to improve a goalkeeper's technique in one specific area of his game, and so technical input will be expected from the coach. Most goalkeeping practices are functional, as repetition increases sound technique, thereby decreasing the chances of making a mistake.

Small-Sided Game (SSG)

The coach must aim to condense down into a small-sided game what is required both technically and tactically. With functional practice, goalkeepers can be opposed or unopposed, but in this situation a lot more tactical work is required from the keeper.

Phase of Play

This is an excellent form of practice, in which the attack or defence for the next game can be planned and the goalkeeper's role can be identified as to what is required in a particular

Drill 59.

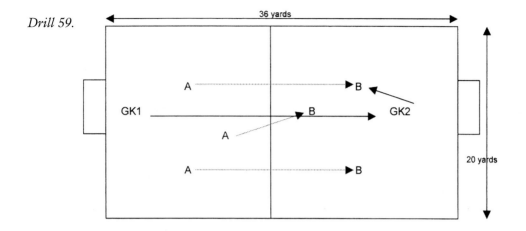

formation of play. This will help to improve the keeper's decision-making during these game situations and improve work situations with the back four. Good understanding between goalkeeper and defenders will achieve more clean sheets, as the needs of both parties can be identified.

Shot-stopping – Small-sided games

Drill 59
2 v 2, 3 v 3 and 4 v 4.

Start:
GK1 throws into GK2, who can roll or play to any of the Bs, who can then score. As soon as GK2 catches, the As can then close down the Bs to prevent them from scoring.

Coaching points:
• starting position
• types of save (i.e., catch, parry, 1 v 1, recovery)
• if parrying – area to aim for, sides of the goal away from attackers approaching towards the ball
• communication – loud, clear and concise
• information – can affect defender closing down, show inside/outside
• position of third defender in 3 v 3
• depth of defenders/compactness
• offside rules apply.

Organizing the session:
• 36yd in length by 20yd width
• footballs in both goals
• offside rules apply/halfway line.

Crossing in a small-sided game

Drill 60
5 v 5 and 6 v 6.

Start:
GK1 throws into GK2, who catches and distributes to one of the As. The Bs now have to keep possession for five passes before the ball can be played out to the wide player, who can cross into the opposite penalty box. Wide right players are asked to cross from deep positions to begin with; this will enable the goalkeeper to work with his defence on their depth and his positioning in relation to the ball and defenders. Servers can change, so the keeper will have to deal with in-swinging and out-swinging crosses as well as by-line crosses from advanced positions.

Progression 6 v 6:
Introduce left-sided players so that the ball can come in from both sides. Once the goalkeepers have caught a cross, they can throw early to wide players.

Drill 60.

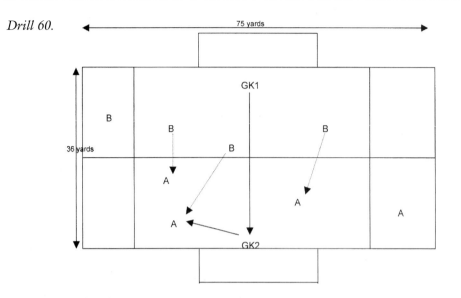

Coaching points:
- goalkeepers' starting position
- depth of defenders
- decision-making – whether the keeper comes for the ball, stays and defends or ets the defenders deal with it
- communication – keeper's or away
- information to defenders if not coming for the cross.

Coaching points – attacking the cross:
- assessment of flight (i.e., angle and speed)
- movement into the ball – timing and attacking at the highest point
- decision-making – catch, punch-height/distance, deflecting and width
- defenders – protect the goal, defend the goal, and attack the ball
- catching – composure and distribution, making an early choice.

Coaching points – not going for the cross:
- defend the goal – positioning and recovery movement
- defenders – compact, squeeze-out and depth
- communication – clear guidelines to defenders.

Dealing with Crosses in a Phase of Play

Drill 61
Start:
Play begins from the middle third with A9, who passes to A1. Once this happens, the Bs defend their goal to stop the cross from passing them. If the goalkeeper catches, he can start play by throwing to the defending team. They have target areas in which to play the ball.

Coaching points:
- Same as crossing in a SSG.

Tactical points:
- middle defending third – show inside/outside
- squeezing out – shape of defenders
- depth of defence – guidelines and where to hold.

Organizing session:
- 60yd by width of pitch
- goalkeeper plus seven players
- seven attackers and two conditioned fullbacks
- fullbacks can only join in when the ball is on their side
- footballs placed around the pitch and target areas coned.
- target areas for defending team to play into.

Drill 61.

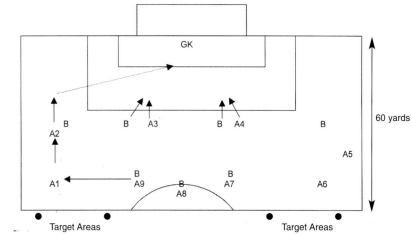

**Dealing with the Back Pass
in a Phase of Play**

Drill 62
Start:
A1 plays the ball to A7, who returns the ball back for A1 to strike over one of the fullbacks. Make sure that the defending team pushes up. B1 plays the ball back to the goalkeeper.

Coaching points:
- goalkeeper's starting position in relation to the ball
- angle and distance of support – whether the goalkeeper needs to make himself available for defenders

- quality of players' back pass
- communication
- composure with ball at keeper's feet
- comfortable with use of both feet
- defenders' adjustment to support goalkeeper
- decision – one or two touch
- selection and choice of pass – wide, central or vision to exploit opposite early (forward)
- goalkeeper's movement once the ball has been played
- range of technique in kicking or throwing.

Tactical points:
- receiving from wide going forward (exploiting)

Drill 62.

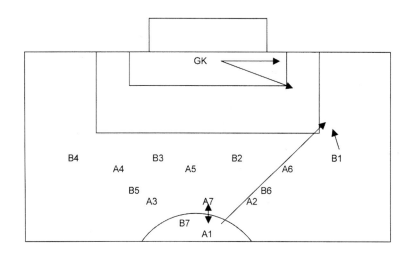

- receiving from central play wide
- receiving from wide to play central
- goalkeeper's vision of his teammates; three-way vision.

Organizing session:

- 60yd by width of pitch
- goalkeeper and seven defenders in bibs
- seven attackers
- target areas are coned.

Distribution in 8 v 8 and 9 v 9 Games

Progression:

- Distribution or dealing with back pass in an 8 v 8 or 9 v 9 playing area becomes 80×60yd. Offside rules apply and normal restarts.

Drill 63

Start:

The Bs play a ball behind the defending As, they pass the ball back to their keeper and play begins. If play breaks down, restart in various positions for both goalkeepers and teammates to deal with.

Coaching points:
- Same as Phase of Play, dealing with back pass
- One acception the goalkeepers may concentrate on all techniques of distributing the ball

Tactical points:
- Same as Phase of Play, dealing with the back pass.

Drill 63.

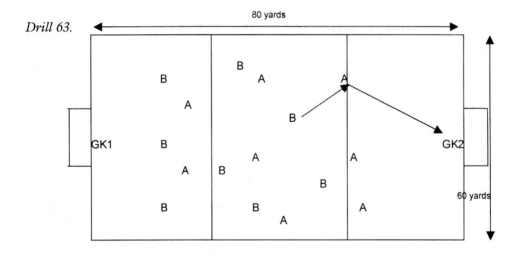

CHAPTER 9

Physical Needs and Conditioning

'The ultimate state for body and mind.'

Goalkeepers require an all-round fitness, as the modern game demands an athletic keeper who is equipped to deal with every challenge that is thrown at him. Therefore, all fitness and conditioning work should be based on what a keeper will do in a realistic game situation. After all, during a game the goalkeeper may be inactive for long periods of time and could then be required to make a save or sprint from his line at speed to make a clearance. Ideally, the fitness work for goalkeeping practices and drills should be specifically anaerobic.

The anaerobic system is the main ingredient of the goalkeeper's conditioning and therefore each drill or practice should last for 30–60sec at a time, with the keeper working at high intensity in short, sharp bursts. The speed at which the keeper works means that oxygen may not be available to produce energy, which is where the ATP (adenosine triphosphate) will regenerate by breaking down the carbohydrates that are stored in the muscles. Even though energy can be reproduced quickly, a substance called lactic acid is formed, which causes fatigue and tiredness in the muscles. By performing anaerobic work in a daily routine, the keeper's movements will become faster and his energy bursts more explosive, which are important reactions and will help the body's ability to recover more quickly after conditioning.

A goalkeeper's fitness requirements are:
• reaction in speed
• agility and power
• endurance speed
• strength.

To maintain peak fitness the keeper must be prepared to work hard, as the skill factor will ultimately break down when fatigue creeps in. This is usually followed by a lack of concentration and mistakes, which will then lead to the goalkeeper underachieving throughout the session. All areas of conditioning should be based on quality, not quantity, so working under pressure should only be part of a balanced weekly schedule.

A goalkeeper's 'no pain, no gain' work ethic should be applied to these types of fitness work. A coach must aim to achieve a purposeful session in order to meet a goalkeeper's individual needs, while also making the session both enjoyable and competitive in

The senior pros at Southampton at work.

order to maintain a healthy rivalry between the keepers. Tests can be regularly carried out to monitor the speed and strength of a goalkeeper's fitness levels.

All goalkeeping coaches are required to inspire and motivate their keepers throughout this type of work. They should also remember to give the keepers adequate periods of rest between fitness practices in order to maintain maximum work levels. Because the anaerobic work of the goalkeeper is power-based, it will help your keeper's speed of reaction when making saves and speed of mind when acting on his decision, carrying it out quickly to produce a positive result.

It could be argued that the duties of protecting goal have increased, what with the new rules of football combined with the keeper working as the fifth defender. It is also important that the goalkeeper's cardiovascular fitness is maintained in line with aerobic levels. This is low-intensity work carried out over long periods, so the keeper should be included in some of the running drills, although specific sessions aimed at increasing a keeper's endurance should also be undertaken.

Younger goalkeepers should concentrate on perfecting all of the techniques, rather than just on conditioning and fitness levels. From the ages of nine to thirteen enjoyment of the game is the main aim, combined with a certain amount of goalkeeping work geared to preparation for the next level of training.

From fourteen onwards, certain conditioning skills should be implemented into a weekly session plan to make sure that fitness levels are balanced with the required technical skills. When a coach is planning conditioning and fitness sessions, certain key factors must always to considered.

Key conditioning and fitness factors are:
• the needs of the goalkeepers, both individually and collectively
• the general fitness of the goalkeeper

• the timing of the session in relation to the season so far and the week ahead
• the type of fitness work.

Following are the target breakdowns for the above areas.

Needs of the Keepers, Individually and Collectively

This will relate to the age and standard of the goalkeepers, whether they are summer school pupils, academy scholars or professional goalkeepers. By identifying the group that you as a coach are working with will help you to organize the appropriate fitness structure to improve personal levels.

General Fitness of the Goalkeeper

Observing your goalkeepers on a weekly basis, during both training sessions and game situations, will help you to evaluate areas that need to be worked on to improve fitness levels. Drills and practice sessions can also be timed and checked to ensure that all areas are being worked to the maximum levels.

Timing of the Session

This will depend on the season, and therefore conditioning should be aimed at

Antti Niemi in full flight at the Staplewood training ground.

What	Basic Fitness	Specific Fitness and Conditioning	Resistance Training
When	Pre-season	Throughout the season depending on games (once a week)	Pre-season 2 x week. In-season 2x week depending on games
How	With the ball, don't overuse power and agility as legs will tire.	Pre season – no ball. In season – with a ball weekly.	Weights/plyometrics with a ball or without. Functional work

maintaining fitness levels throughout the year. Coaches must also note that intense work too close to a game can result in the goalkeeper feeling tired and fatigued, therefore careful planning is required in line with games and travelling arrangements in order to maintain a keeper's freshness.

Type of Fitness Work

Age consideration is an important factor when planning fitness work and an overall picture should be identified and implemented for the keepers' specific requirements. Remember that after the warm-up and stretching exercises, you should continue with the fast and explosive work, leaving the speed and endurance work to the end of the session. Always consider the ground conditions before setting up the session.

Organization of any session can be targeted by using the WHAT, WHEN and HOW guidelines outlined above.

The following section is designed to help in the achievement of goalkeeping fitness, which is a vital part of becoming an excellent technician.

Reaction in Speed

This is an important area for all goalkeepers. There are three main aspects, all of which should be addressed during training sessions.

SPEED OF REACTION

Speed of reaction is the ability to re-adjust and change direction to make a save at the last moment. This covers deflected shots, recovery saves, spreading/blocking saves and even dealing with a misjudged back pass.

SPEED OF BODY

Speed of body covers the keeper's movements across the goal into the line of the ball and down the line. It includes all speed techniques – backwards, forwards and lateral movements, 1 v 1 situations, shot-stopping, far-post crosses, punching, short back pass, and the role of the sweeper–keeper.

SPEED OF MIND

This is the most important aspect, as all the other elements are non-effective without this. Is the keeper able to predict situations and can he adapt to deal with any difficulty that arises during a game?

The following drills are aimed at improving a keeper's speed in all three areas.

Drill 64

The goalkeeper starts on one of the posts; six footballs are placed diagonally out to the edge of the six-yard box, three either side. On the coach's command, starting with the balls nearest to the goal area the keeper must touch every ball as quickly as possible, moving from one side to the other. This can be timed and monitored.

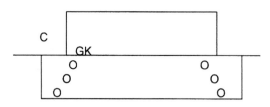

Drill 64

Drill 65

Two cones are placed 4yd apart, in a full-sized goal. The goalkeeper, facing into the goal, has to roll the ball through his legs, spin and save a shot from S1. If the keeper deflects the ball in a good area away from the goal, then praise is due. If the parry is out to S1, then S1 must react appropriately. S2 and S3 supply the keeper with balls if required. Eight to ten reps.

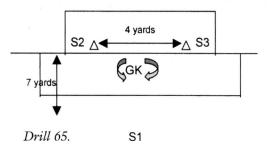

Drill 65.   S1

Drill 66

The goalkeeper is placed in the goal with the server on the eighteen-yard box. The coach dictates which position the keeper must adopt in the goal. On the coach's call, the keeper must regain a starting position to make a save or catch. Eight to ten reps.

STRENGTH

All goalkeepers will undoubtedly need strength in their game, and so strength-building exercises should be incorporated as part of the weekly sessions. There will be a steady progression in younger keepers as they grow and change physically. Strong upper and lower limbs are required for all goalkeepers as they must be able to withstand challenges from all directions.

These practices are designed to help build strength, while at the same time helping to lift and move a keeper's body weight around the goal area.

Drill 67

The coach stands behind the goal; two cones are placed on the six-yard line and another 6yd away. The keeper starts at the furthest cone, and as he jogs to the second cone the coach serves the ball over the crossbar. The keeper attacks the ball, aiming to catch it above the bar. Once caught, he touches the ground with the ball and, springing back up with a double-footed push, returns the ball back over to the coach. He then retreats backwards quickly to the second cone, goes around it and begins again from the other side. Six reps.

Note: This drill is demanding on the backs and fronts of the legs.

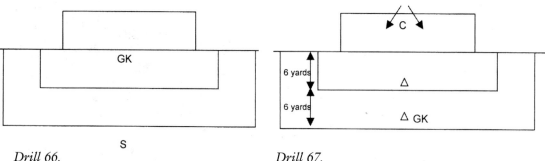

Drill 66.   *Drill 67.*

Strength of Spring

Drill 68

The goalkeeper is in the middle of the goal, adopting a half-squat position. On the coach's command, the keeper must react to the ball, which is being thrown to either side of him, and make the save. Six to eight reps.

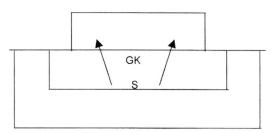

Drill 68.

Strength of Abdomen

Drill 69

The keeper sits on the ground and the server stands 3yd away and serves the ball either side of the keeper for him to catch and return. Twenty reps.

Note: This practice is fine for younger keepers, but reduce the quantity and intensity.

Alan Blayney works with the author on strengthening the abdomen area.

Strength of Arms

Drill 70

This is a variation of the press-up drill and is aimed at improving upper body strength. It can be implemented within any conditioning session:

- press-ups on one ball, both hands
- press-ups on one ball, but now changing hands
- press-ups on two balls
- press-ups without a ball; make a triangle with thumbs and index fingers (when doing this drill try to aim to put your nose in the triangle of your hands).

The age and physical condition of the keeper is revealed in this practice, so encourage the keeper to increase the number weekly, even if it is only by one a week.

AGILITY

This is needed by all goalkeepers so that they can climb and make the impossible top corner saves. Being fluent in movement and balance will help in this area, and will also help when changing direction in flight. Flexibility is paramount, as the keeper will need to push

his body continually and be versatile and adaptable at short notice.

These practices are aimed at helping to improve a goalkeeper's instinctive reactions, sharpness and agility across the goal.

Drill 71

The goalkeeper stands facing four balls; the coach plays each ball low to the keeper's right for him to save. This is repeated from both left and right of the goal. A variation on this practice is for the coach to throw high, again from the left and right of the goal.

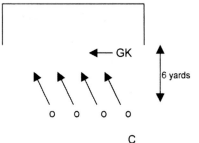

Drill 71.

Drill 72

GK1 is placed 2yd from the goal line and GK2 stands behind him. On the coach's call, GK1 bends for GK2 to leap-frog him; the server can either throw, volley or half-volley to either side of the keeper to make the save. This session can be reversed so that GK2 goes through the legs of GK1 to make a save. Timing from the server is important for this practice. Six reps max.

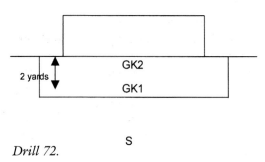

Drill 72.

Drill 73.

The keeper is positioned lying on the ground facing the server with his arms outstretched. The server throws the ball to the keeper, who catches and throws back to the server, and on doing so uses the throw to get himself to his feet and save a throw from the server on the opposite side. Once saved, the process starts again from the opposite side. Six reps in total.

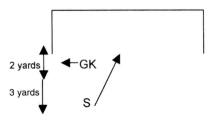

Drill 73.

Power

While most of the keeper's work is anaerobic, he also needs to have the ability to expend energy in short, sharp powerful explosions. The muscles contract when they are trying to shorten, but as the length increases, this creates explosive power for the goalkeeper to react quickly. This is also known as plyometrics, a system of exercise that helps the body to store and use energy in relation to the way the keeper works. For example, a keeper might have to make a low save, which he might only parry and then have to react high to the follow-up shot.

A well-structured programme is needed when using plyometrics, as poor or insufficient preparation increases the risk of injury. Always ensure that the warm-up and stretches are carried out properly. Plyometric work will not leave you out of breath or tired, but muscle soreness twenty-four hours later can occur as a result of lack of preparation.

A general guide for using plyometrics:
- do not use 24-48hr before a game
- the intensity must be sufficient to achieve an overload
- rest is vital between each set
- increase work progressively
- if muscle soreness develops end the session immediately
- speed, effort and technique should be paramount when using maximum actions to the full
- be aware of the number of ground contacts when working any muscle group; the number should depend on experience, age and build, but should not exceed 120
- sessions should only apply to sixteen years and above
- work to the biological age of goalkeepers and not their chronological age.

The ball is an ideal tool to use for these exercises, as it makes the work both enjoyable and effective, adding additional benefits and enhanced results.

Drill 74
A box shape is made from hurdles. The keeper begins by jumping over the first hurdle, then taking one bounce before jumping the second hurdle into position 1. He jumps back into the centre before jumping into position 2 and back again, repeating the process and finishing at position 3. The coach is looking for a total of twelve contacts with the ground during the jumps.

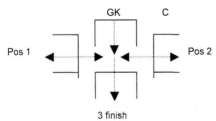

Drill 74.

The next practice is aimed at getting the keeper to achieve fewer contacts, which will mean a more dynamic and powerful jump. Aim for six contacts. On a rotational basis each practice should be achieved four times, starting with forty-eight contacts, and in the second down to just twenty-four contacts, and so on.

Drill 75
The keeper stands 2yd from the line and jumps, bringing his knees to his chest. On landing, the coach serves the ball to the left or right for the keeper to dive and catch. This is repeated four times, twice either side. Perform on a rotational system with the other keepers increasing the number of jumps.

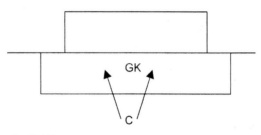

Drill 75.

One – knee to chest   ×4 saves = contacts ×4
Two – knee to chest   ×4 saves = contacts ×8
Three – knee to chest   ×4 saves = contacts ×12
Four – knee to chest   ×4 saves = contacts ×16

Total contacts in set = 40

Drill 76
Server stands 8yd away and on his command the keeper laterally jumps the hurdle, and on contact returns straight away and moves into a low shot from the server. This is repeated four times, creating eight contacts. After a rest this is repeated with the keeper working high, left and right, making a total of thirty-two contacts.

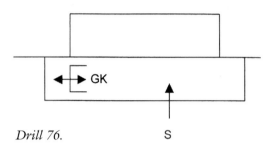

Drill 76.

SPEED ENDURANCE

This last section shows ways in which goal-keepers can retain their endurance in situations that relate to the movements they make during a game.

This work is kept until the end of the keeper's session and while the coach will want the keeper to work hard, the session should still retain quality. Speed endurance work should also contain elements to increase the removal of lactic acid, thereby reducing the keeper's recovery time after intense work. Goalkeepers work in specific ways and therefore can be excused some of the running, as long as they have a programme that will improve their overall endurance.

Drill 77

The goalkeeper is positioned in the middle of the goal with the server 10yd away. The keeper moves as quickly as he can, gliding around each cone to make a low save. The keeper must complete this task as quickly as possible and must deal with each individual shot. Repeat this exercise from both left and right of the goal. Four reps each side.

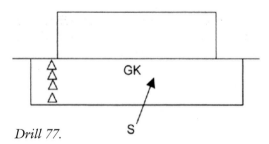

Drill 77.

Progression

This exercise can be executed as high saves, but instead of gliding around each cone the keeper now knocks each cone over before making the save.

Drill 78

The goalkeeper lays down facing the server, who is 4yd away. The server throws the ball for the keeper to dive and catch. On landing, the keeper throws the ball back to the server from the floor. The server then returns the ball for the keeper to make another save. This is repeated six times to the right and then six times to the left.

Drill 78.

Drill 79

The goalkeeper starts in the middle of the goal and S1 starts by side-footing the ball low for the keeper to make a save. Once he has made the save he must get to his feet and face a ball from S2, who serves high. This service is repeated for six balls, working low one side and high the other. Once finished, reverse the practice in order to work high and low from both sides.

Remember – quality service will create quality goalkeepers. As a coach, remember that while constructive criticism never hurt anyone, praise is a stronger morale-boosting tool for all keepers during conditioning work.

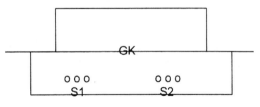

Drill 79.

CHAPTER 10

Final Thoughts and Summary

'You are only as good as your last game.'

Even the best goalkeepers make mistakes – unfortunately it goes with the job that you have chosen. Being able to deal with mistakes in a game and not let them affect the rest of your performance is always difficult, but it is part of the mental strength you must acquire as a goalkeeper. After all, no goalkeeper enters the field with negative thoughts.

The saying 'you are only as good as your last game' really does apply to the role of a goalkeeper. If you make one mistake it seems that everyone will remember it, and the saves and decisions you make to keep your team in the game are not always recognized or remembered. Being able to deal with mistakes is not an easy process and it adds pressure to up and coming young keepers; if they are unable to cope with this aspect of the game it is unlikely they will be able to maximize their full potential.

A coach's role is to understand and support the goalkeeper by evaluating his faults either during games or training. Training is without doubt an important aspect of a coach's job, as it is a fantastic tool with which to rebuild your keepers' confidence and belief in their own abilities. A structured, continuous coaching programme should be implemented by all goalkeeping coaches, based on sound techniques and demonstrations, which should be fully explained in detail so as to form a good grounding from which youngsters can learn.

Good observation skills and diagnoses of faults are qualities that all coaches should possess, together with a sound knowledge of the keeper's role. Coaching styles should vary so that the needs of both experienced and inexperienced keepers are met. An organized coach will be able to influence his keepers by preparing a well-structured training programme that hopefully motivates and inspires them to succeed to the highest level.

Training should be productive in terms of content and stimulation, to the point where you are asking questions of your keepers in relation to realistic ideas. Constructive criticism, if backed-up with solid foundations of fact, technique, decision-making and demonstrations, is a valuable learning tool, if required. However, motivation and praise are the biggest stimulants the coach can have in his glove bag.

My closing thoughts are that there can only be one place on a Saturday for a goalkeeper, but remember that there will always be another keeper waiting in the wings for their chance at your position. All goalkeepers will come across this situation, whether it is through injury, loss of form or the manager's choice. Even though rivalry is healthy between keepers, it will always be difficult for the coach to make sure that the one who is not playing still feels just as important and still part of the squad. The non-playing keeper must be prepared both mentally and physically to mount a challenge for the number one slot and to take the position if the opportunity presents itself.

There is nothing more satisfying than when a goalkeeper achieves a clean sheet without errors, or enjoys a game where he is unbeatable in all departments. Only then can he reflect on a week of hard work, preparation and total application on a job well done by a specialist.

Always observe and learn from the top-class goalkeepers – watch for the various attributes each keeper possesses, but remember that you cannot base your own game on theirs. The young goalkeeper should create his own style of goalkeeping based on his strengths and abilities. All teenagers will grow at different speeds, so it is important that as goalkeepers all areas of their game, both their strengths and weaknesses, are worked on constantly to achieve a consistent approach. Coaches are unable to do anything about genetics, so when a smaller keeper is performing without errors, height is unimportant.

The hardest part of my job as a goalkeeping coach is turning away young hopefuls due to the fact that we already have an allotted number of keepers in any particular age group, or that they are just not up to the existing standard. If you are a young keeper, you must continue to believe in your abilities and work on any weak areas to prepare for that next opportunity. Try not to become disheartened if you are turned down by an academy or club, as all young keepers, as explained throughout the book, develop at different stages, and your chance may still come.

> For the lucky ones, there is no substitute for skill and technique – they are a gift. But they are only gained through sheer hard work to reach the top and stay there !

Don't miss the follow on from this book – a DVD is now in the planning stages and should be available in early 2004.

For further information or to contact David Coles e-mail: Colesys@keepers2003.freeserve.co.uk

A debrief is very important for feedback on the keeper's work.

Index

INDEX